BOOKS BY DOROTHY NAFUS MORRISON

Can I Help How I Feel?
(*with Carl V. Morrison*)

Ladies Were Not Expected
Abigail Scott Dunniway and Women's Rights

The Eagle and the Fort
The Story of John McLaughlin

Chief Sarah
Sarah Winnemucca's Fight for Indian Rights

CHIEF SARAH

Sarah Winnemucca's Fight for Indian Rights

Dorothy Nafus Morrison

CHIEF SARAH

Sarah Winnemucca's Fight for Indian Rights

ILLUSTRATED WITH OLD PRINTS AND
PHOTOGRAPHS AND WITH MAPS

Atheneum 1980 New York

The photograph by Timothy O'Sullivan that appears on the
jacket back and on pages 70 and 71 is from
America's Forgotten Photographer, Timothy O'Sullivan
by James D. Horan, published by Doubleday.

LIBRARY OF CONGRESS CATALOGING IN PUBLICATION DATA

Morrison, Dorothy N   Chief Sarah.

Bibliography: p. 161
Includes index.
SUMMARY: A biography of the Paiute Indian woman
scout, lecturer, author, educator, and lobbyist
who has been called the Indian Joan of Arc because
of her efforts to gain and protect the rights of
her people.
1. Hopkins, Sarah Winnemucca, 1844?-1891—
Juvenile literature. 2. Paiute Indians—Biography
—Juvenile literature. [1. Hopkins, Sarah
Winnemucca, 1844?-1891. 2. Paiute Indians—
Biography. 3. Indians of North America—
Biography] I. Title.
E99.P2H725   970'.004'97   79-22545
ISBN 0-689-30752-7

Published simultaneously in Canada by
McClelland & Stewart, Ltd.
Manufactured by American Book-Stratford Press, Inc
Saddle Brook, New Jersey
Designed by M. M. Ahern
First Edition

For Carl
Always

Contents

vii

Author's Note

I FIRST RAN ACROSS the name of Sarah Winnemucca while doing research about some other people in the West, and once I had read of her adventures, I could never forget them. So I decided to write this book.

One of my best aids was her autobiography, *Life Among the Piutes: Their Wrongs and Claims.* She wrote it from memory—but what a memory! The more I checked it against official reports, newspapers and other sources, the more I was amazed. Some of her accounts seemed too dreadful to be true—yet they were supported in detail by sober government documents. She made some mistakes, especially in dates, which had little meaning for a dweller in the timeless desert, and she didn't always understand the machinery of federal bureaus. But she had a true story, which she told honestly and well. I have here repeated many conversations just as Sarah remembered and wrote them. I made up nothing. The truth is more exciting than any fiction.

In comparing Sarah's book with other sources, I found two major points to question. For the incident of the Washoe arrows, in Chapter One, Sarah listed three prisoners, while the Sacramento *Daily Union* of 1857, in items spread over five months, said only one was brought in, the other two having escaped. Since Sarah was there, while the reporter was more than one hundred miles away and had to rely on chance travelers for information, I have accepted the number she gave. The important thing is that in the main they agreed.

The other question was the time of Captain Truckee's death, which some place shortly after the Pyramid Lake War, while she says it was before. However, a number of warriors who fought there were interviewed and named many chiefs from that war without mentioning Truckee. Also, the later date is based on a California newspaper of 1875—fifteen years after the war, too long to be reliable. So I have followed Sarah's version. Again, she was there.

Early white writers spelled Indian names in various ways. Thus Paiute was "Piute"—or "Pah-Ute"—or "Pahute." For all these I have used the common modern spellings, except in quotations.

Members of Sarah's family were also given various names. Her father was called "Old Winnemucca," or "Winnemucca II," or simply "Winnemucca." Her cousin Numaga was sometimes called "Young Winnemucca," and another chief, Naana, was known as "Little Winnemucca." Some writers called her grandfather "Winnemucca I," and Natchez was occasionally referred to as "Winnemucca." To clear away this confusion, I have followed the accepted modern usage of Winnemucca for Sarah's father, Numaga for her cousin, the war chief, Captain Truckee for her grandfather, and Natchez for her brother.

One of the pleasures of an author is meeting friendly people. In Nevada, the staffs of the State Library, State Museum, Historical Society, and University Library, all shared knowledge and materials. Ferol Egan answered some puzzling questions. Margaret Wheat supplied pictures from her outstanding collection and advice from her vast store of knowledge, and Carrie Townley helped eliminate mistakes. Others, who furnished pictures, are listed on the page of credits. To all of them, my sincere thanks.

I am also grateful to the staff of Multnomah Library in Portland, Oregon, especially to the Interlibrary Loan Service, for patiently securing stacks of microfilms plus much printed material.

Without such assistance, I couldn't have written this book.

CHIEF SARAH

Sarah Winnemucca's
Fight for
Indian Rights

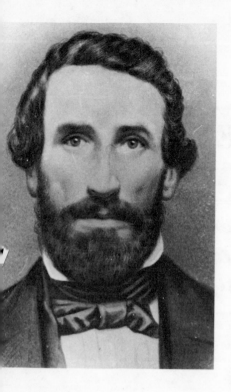

Major William Ormsby, in whose home Sarah and Elma
lived. NEVADA HISTORICAL SOCIETY

Mrs. Margaret Ormsby, Major Ormsby's wife. She was
probably the one who first taught Sarah to read and write.
NEVADA STATE MUSEUM

ONE

Sarah Speaks Out
1857

HOOFBEATS POUNDED the desert floor. They were faint at first but grew rapidly louder until they resounded from the nearby mountains and rolled through the single dusty street of the frontier town, Genoa, Nevada. Hearing them, Sarah Winnemucca— daughter of a chief, sister of a chief—knew there was going to be trouble. Two white men had been murdered, arrows had been found in the wounds, and Major Ormsby had sent for Sarah's people, the Paiutes.

Sarah and her sister Elma had lived in Genoa with Major Ormsby's family for a whole year, sent by their grandfather to learn the white man's ways. Still, Sarah was loyal to her tribe, and the thud of hoofs filled her with dread. It was September, 1857, when she was about thirteen years old.

She went outside the Ormsby house to watch the warriors draw close. Her brother Natchez, the peace chief, and her cousin Numaga, the war chief, rode in the lead, and when they drew rein, with a shout from their followers, Major Ormsby stepped forward.

He was tall and excitable, with short black chin whiskers, and as he spoke, Sarah's face burned with embarrassment, for he didn't follow the rules of Indian courtesy. He didn't inquire about the chiefs' health, or offer to smoke together, giving each time to look into the other's face and see into his heart. He didn't even make a polite comment on the weather. Instead, he handed over the fatal arrows.

"Do you know what tribe these arrows belong to?" he demanded harshly in English, which Sarah understood well.

Numaga, tall and broad-shouldered, with wary, deepset eyes, turned them over in his hand. "The Washoes," he replied in his deep voice.

"Will you help us get the Washoe chief to give up the men who killed the whites?" asked Ormsby, his tone making it a command.

Sarah gasped. Surely he knew that the Washoes and Paiutes were not friends, that the only reason they didn't go to war was because it took all their energy to find food in their dry land! Surely he knew better than to send chiefs as errand boys to their enemies!

But, Numaga grimly overlooked the insult and chose five men to bring in the Washoe leader. This was his only honorable course, for the Paiutes and whites had made a treaty in which both promised to turn over wrong-doers of either race.

That night, Sarah watched the first war dance she had ever seen performed by her peace-loving people. Yet peace seemed to be slipping away from them. Many white men were passing through the desert on the trail to the California gold fields, while others had come to stay. Some of them were kind. A few—the cruel ones— burned the Numa's caches of stored food and shot the Indians on sight. Sarah was in turmoil, loving her people, yet loving the Ormsbys too; frightened, yet thrilled as she tried to spot Natchez and Numaga among the painted warriors by the bonfire.

Several days later Captain Jim of the Washoes came in, an enormous man, bear-like in his rabbit-skin robe, wearing a necklace of bones. "You ask me if these are my people's arrows. I say yes," rumbled Captain Jim in the Washoe tongue. Natchez was interpreter, but even without him Sarah could understand, for she was unusually quick at languages.

The major turned toward Natchez. "Tell Captain Jim that his people have killed two men, and he must bring them in. They shall not be hurt. All will be right."

"I know my people have not killed the men," Captain Jim protested. "None have been away; we are all at Pine-Nut Valley."

But the major brusquely told Captain Jim he must surrender the murderers or the Paiutes would make war on them, for they and the whites were friends. "Now go and bring them in," he ordered.

Although Sarah pitied the Washoes as they walked away looking at the ground, Major Ormsby had promised they would not be hurt, and Natchez had repeated his words. Surely, as the major said, all would be right.

Captain Jim had no choice. Unless he surrendered someone—anyone—the whites would make a war that might wipe out his whole band. Therefore, in mid-October he again appeared, bringing three frightened young prisoners, along with their mothers, one young wife, and several others of his tribe. Quickly the whites bound the young men's wrists and locked them up, and the next morning, when they were led out, a crowd gathered. Sarah, her sister Elma, and the Ormsby family were there.

"Hang the red devils right off!" shouted someone in the crowd, while boys threw stones and jeered.

When thirty-one men appeared with guns on their shoulder, a Washoe woman began to scream, "Oh, they have come to kill them!"

All the women flung themselves on Natchez. "Oh, dear chieftain, they did not kill the white men—indeed they did not. They have not been away from our camp for over a month." They said Captain Jim had chosen these three because they had no fathers to protect them and no children to need them.

"Oh, Good Spirit, come!" prayed the young wife. "Come into the hearts of this people. Oh, whisper in their hearts that they may not kill my poor husband!" She spoke to Natchez. "Our cruel chief has given up my husband because he is afraid we will all be killed."

Bound by the treaty, Natchez folded his arms and explained that the men were only going to be taken to California to be tried. But the terrified prisoners had so little faith in the white man's justice that they tried to run away. Instantly the settlers raised their guns and fired, killing two and recapturing the third, who was wounded and soon died.

The young wife threw herself on the dead body of her husband; the mothers took their bleeding sons into their arms. "Oh, my sweet son—gone, gone!" wailed one.

Such grief, Sarah thought, was enough to make the very mountain weep. It was cruel, and wrong, for the major had promised that the young warriors would not be harmed. Natchez, who had repeated the major's words, had been betrayed.

Brilliant, sensitive, with a scorching temper, Sarah was outraged at the broken promise. She turned toward Mrs. Ormsby.

"I believe those Washoe women. They say their men are all innocent," she exclaimed, as tears streamed down her face. "They say they were not away from their camp for a long time." She told Mrs. Ormsby all she had heard the women say, and repeated many times, "I believe them. I believe them."

Mrs. Ormsby drew back. "How came the Washoe arrows there? And the chief himself has brought them to us. My husband knows what he is doing." Gentle as she had been in the past, today she showed no pity.

Sarah then went to her brother and the Washoe

Captain Jim of the Washoe tribe as an old man. NEVADA
HISTORICAL SOCIETY

chief. "It is I who have killed them," Captain Jim was saying, his voice heavy with sorrow. "Their blood is on my hands."

Slowly the crowd dispersed, leaving the Washoes with their dead.

For Sarah and Elma this was a shattering experience. Elma fell sick. Neither one could bear to stay in Genoa, nor did their family want them to. As soon as Elma was well enough, Natchez and several warriors took them to their own people, to live once more in a brush *karnee* and wander over the desert in search of food.

SEVERAL WEEKS LATER, on a cold winter day, a huge man stepped close to their fire, where melting snow dripped from his robe and ran down his broad face. It was Captain Jim, come to say the Washoes had not been guilty. Instead, two white men had done the killing and placed arrows in the wounds to throw blame onto the Indians.

"Who told you?" asked Natchez.

"Major Ormsby says so," Captain Jim replied, and explained that the men had been gambling, got into a fight, and boasted about the murders. Drawing his robe around him Natchez then followed the Washoe chief out into the storm, to travel to the settlement and see for himself what had happened.

Left behind, Sarah thought about that autumn day at Genoa—the readiness of the settlers to shoot first and find out the truth afterward—Major Ormsby's rudeness

—his promise broken as lightly as a man would snap a twig. Had the chiefs been right in keeping to their treaty? Or had they been wrong in helping capture innocent Washoes? Could they find any honorable course in these troubled days?

Sarah remembered how boldly she had thrown herself into the arms of Mrs. Ormsby and protested that the weeping Washoe women told the truth. Few Indians, and especially young Indian girls, would talk so to the wife of a white man.

But Sarah belonged to a family of chiefs.

TWO

Like a Roaring Lion
1844–1851

SARAH HAD NOT always been so brave. When she was small, she was terrified of the white men who sometimes passed through Nevada, for she heard her people say they had "something like awful thunder and lightning," and came "like a roaring lion," shooting the Indians on sight.

Sarah had been born about 1844 in the Great Basin, a dry land of towering mountains and flat valleys that wound on and on between the ridges, farther than she could see, farther than she had ever gone, past the horizon and beyond. It was called a "basin" because its rivers ran inward to lakes and marshes instead of outward to the ocean. Living there, Sarah was used to the glare of sun on rocks and sand, mirages, fierce cold winds in winter, whirls of dust that stung her face, stars like lamps in the black desert night.

Except for the fearsome white men, her childhood was happy. The Indians of the Great Basin were kind to their young, never striking them, but guiding them through love and reasoning.

"My people teach their children never to make fun of anyone, no matter how they look," she later wrote. "If you see your brother or sister doing something wrong, look away, or go away from them. If you make fun of bad persons, you make yourself beneath them."

She began each day by washing her face in clear cold water, facing the sunrise, and praying to the Spirit-Father. Before each meal she offered part of the food to the earth in thanksgiving.

These Indians didn't call themselves Paiutes, but Numa, the People, the name "Pah-ute" being given later, possibly from a Numa word meaning water. They were not a large, organized tribe, but lived in small groups, each with its head man, and Sarah felt important because her grandfather led her branch.

Since they had few horses, the Numa trudged on foot over the Great Basin, seeking food. Sometimes Sarah lived near shallow Honey Lake; sometimes at the "sink" of the Humboldt River, where it flattens out into a marsh and sinks into the soil; sometimes at Pyramid Lake—sacred, blue and green, mysterious between its bare, brown hills. She learned to cut armloads of rice-

Paiute woman gathering *tules* (bulrushes) from the marshy edge of Pyramid Lake. Tules, grass and cattails were used in making many articles, such as baskets, cradleboards and clothing. MARGARET WHEAT

grass, to collect cattail pollen for cakes, to split and dry fish, and to build *karnees*, huts woven of sage brush or cattails. In the fall, she plodded high up into the mountains to collect pine nuts. The Paiutes worked hard, but they played too, for they loved games, races and gambling, and since they always shared with anyone in need, gambling didn't harm them.

In spring the desert bloomed. Most girls were named for flowers, and at the Flower Festival each would make up songs about her own name. Sarah's was the Indian word for shellflower.

My name is Thocmetony.
I shall be beautiful while the earth lasts.
Who will come and be happy with me in the Spirit-land?
I shall be beautiful forever there. . . .
Come, oh come, and dance and be happy with me!

The young men sang too, dancing beside the girls.

Sarah adored her grandfather, who had faith in a Paiute legend. It said that in the beginning of the world there was a family with four children, one dark girl and boy, one light girl and boy. For a time they got along well, but later they quarreled.

"Why are you so cruel to each other?" their father sorrowfully asked, at which they hung their heads in shame. But they continued to quarrel until at last he said, "Depart from each other, you cruel children. Go across the mighty ocean and do not seek each other's lives."

So the dark girl and boy disappeared and grew into the large nation of Indians, while the light girl and boy grew into another large nation of whites. One day, said the legend, the white nation would send someone to the Indians to heal the trouble.

Believing this, Sarah's grandfather called the white men his brothers. When Sarah was very small, he and several other Numa became guides to Captain John

Charles Fremont, going all the way to California, where they aided Fremont in the Mexican War. The soldiers called her grandfather Captain Truckee, which is the Numa word for "very good."

On their return Captain Truckee and his men brought guns that were so loud the children screamed at every shot. Sarah was afraid to go to his camp and fought and bit her mother. "Oh, mother, mother, don't take us there!" she cried in terror.

However, she soon made friends with her grandfather, and listened as he sat for days describing the wonderful things he had seen in California—beautiful clothes, "big houses that go on the mighty ocean and travel faster than any horse," "moving houses" (wagons), and a gun that could shoot a ball larger than his head.

Fremont had given him a note of recommendation, which Captain Truckee called his "rag friend." "This can talk to all our white brothers, and our white sisters and their children," he said. "It can go and talk with their fathers and brothers and sisters and come back to tell what they are doing." The rag friend brought Truckee great respect from both settlers and Indians, but Sarah was afraid of its mysterious power.

There was also fear among many of the other Numa because of friends who had been killed by whites, often without cause. "Oh, our great chieftain," said the medicine men and women, "we are afraid your white brothers will yet make your people's hearts bleed. Their blood is all around us, and the dead are lying all about us, and we cannot escape it. It will come."

Terrified, little Sarah listened to every word.

One winter the Indians heard about a party of immigrants who were caught in mountain blizzards and at last hadn't anything to eat except the flesh of those who died. After that Numa mothers would tell their children that if they were not good, the settlers would come and eat them up. Sarah's father, on a fishing trip to the Humboldt River, saw his first white men. When he came back to his people hiding among the mountains, he said the strangers were not like humans but owls, because they had hair on their faces and had white (meaning blue, or light) eyes. Sarah couldn't bear to think of the owl-faced creatures who might eat her.

One hot, windy day, word came that white people were near, so she and her family ran away. Her aunt was helping a little cousin, while her mother tried to carry baby Elma on her back and drag Sarah along by the hand, but the frightened children could hardly move their feet. They were so slow that at last their mothers scraped out shallow holes in the loose soil and hid Sarah and her cousin by partly covering them with earth and shielding them with sage brush. Then they ran away with the rest.

Sketch of Pyramid Lake from the report of Captain John Charles Fremont, who discovered the lake in early 1844 and named it for the massive rock island in this sketch. When he traveled on to California, Captain Truckee accompanied him. AUTHOR

The children had to wait alone all day, wondering every second whether the owl-faced men were near. Sometimes they whispered, but softly—softly—so no one could hear. Shadows moved. Scorpions, mice, horned toads and yellow-backed lizards skittered past. Every moment Sarah feared she might be found and eaten.

"Oh, father, have you forgotten me?" she murmured. "Are you never coming for me?"

At dark, when she heard whispering and footsteps, she thought her heart would jump right out of her mouth. Then her mother's voice said, " 'Tis right here!" And at last she and her cousin were uncovered. Forever afterward, she remembered the terror of that day when she had felt buried alive.

In 1849, when Sarah was about five, gold was discovered in California, bringing hordes of white men across the Great Basin—prospectors, adventurers, storekeepers, and an occasional farmer who settled on Paiute land. Sarah didn't see them, because her people fled, but she heard about them. She knew that some were friendly, while others let their stock eat the meadow grass, set fire to the caches of pine nuts that were stored for winter, and shot the Indians without cause. Although a few hungry Paiutes stole food and cattle, most of them were peaceful and honest, and the troublemakers were generally from tribes from farther east. Even so, some immigrants hated and feared all Indians, good or bad, gentle or cruel.

One day, in the year after California gold was discovered, Sarah's father, grandfather, uncles, and other Paiutes were peacefully fishing on the Humboldt River when white men fired on them, killing Sarah's uncle and five others. Her aunt, mother, and father cut off their hair and made gashes in their arms and legs, for that was the way the Paiutes mourned. Furious, the Numa held council after council at which they made wild plans to get revenge by murdering the settlers.

Captain Truckee refused. "How dare you ask me to let your hearts be stained with the blood of those who are innocent of the deed that has been done to us by others?" he said. "Is not my dear beloved son laid alongside of your dead, and you say I stand up for their lives . . . I know and you know that those men who live at the sink are not the ones that killed our men."

He wept as he talked. Everyone wept, until Sarah could hardly hear his words. But he insisted that the only way the Numa could survive was to keep peace with the settlers.

The settlers! Sarah shivered. The white-eyes! The owl-faces! She hoped she would never have to see them.

THAT SAME FALL Captain Truckee told his family that he wanted them to learn the ways of his white brothers. Since he knew men in the settlements who would give them work, he planned to take thirty families to California, leaving Sarah's father, Winnemucca, to act as chief, but including Sarah with her mother, brothers and sisters in the move. When Captain Truckee told his plan, the women pleaded to remain at home,

Two Paiute women in an early photograph. One has a burden basket on her back and is holding a flat winnowing basket which she will use to toss seeds or nuts into the air, in order to blow out the chaff. MUSEUM OF THE AMERICAN INDIAN, HEYE FOUNDATION

and Sarah listened in horror. Surely, surely, her dear, kind grandfather would not make them go against their will. But Captain Truckee was firm.

Fearfully, those who were to make the trip gathered everything they would need. By now Truckee's band had acquired horses, so Sarah was boosted up behind her big brother Natchez and hung on with both chubby fists. Shutting her eyes, she buried her face against the soft fur of his robe.

She was on her way to meet the owl-faced men.

THREE

The Owl-Faced Men
1851–1852

SARAH WAS a fiery little girl. Whenever they passed a settler's home, she hid her face in her brother's robe, and if he refused to cover her, she screamed, scratched him and bit him on his back. When whites approached, she danced around "like a wild creature," hid behind her mother, and peeping out and seeing their hairy faces, she screamed, "Oh, mother, the owls!" Nearing a settlement, she fought, kicked, bit her mother, and cried in terror. She wasn't the only frightened one. Her big brother Natchez cried at first, too.

Most settlers were Mormons, for at that time

Nevada was part of Utah Territory. Wherever they went, Captain Truckee would show his rag friend, at which the white people would smile and often give them presents. Sarah liked the strange bread and beef, but she was still timid. When the rest of the Numa received red shirts and calico dresses, she didn't get anything because she was hiding under some robes. Offered sugar, she held out her hand for it, but didn't look up.

"Let us go back to Father—let us not go with Grandpa, for he is bad," she coaxed, although she loved Captain Truckee.

"We can't go alone," her mother replied. "We would all be killed, for we have no rag friend."

Holding both hands over her face and crying as if her heart would break, Sarah heard her grandfather's voice. "Well, well, is my sweetheart never going to stop crying?" he gently asked. "Come, I have something for my baby. Come and see what it is."

Sarah went to him then, with her head down, and he gave her a little cup which, he explained, was to drink water from, not to wear as an ornament. Chuckling, he told her about the first gift he had received from the soldiers—a tin plate, which he proudly fastened to his head for a hat. Even though Sarah's cup was a treasure, she still lay awake many nights, imagining the owl-faces with their pale, cold eyes.

Following the Humboldt and then the Carson River, they left the Great Basin, rode up and up to the summit of the Sierras, and camped in snow that fell all night, heavy on the trees. On the other side of the

A Paiute woman with her papoose in a cradle board. She is wearing a skirt made of grass or rushes. AUTHOR

mountains they rode through Sacramento Valley to Stockton, where Captain Truckee's friend lived in a "very big house made of red stone"—probably brick. It was high, so high, thought Sarah, as she marveled at the stairs.

Here she had a new treat—cake—which she liked so well that she ate a great deal of it, and fell ill.

"The sugar-bread was poisoned, which your white brother gave us to eat, and it has made my poor little girl so sick that I am afraid she will die," her mother said.

"Dear daughter," Captain Truckee replied. "I am sorry you have such a bad heart against my white brothers. I have eaten some sugar-bread, and so have you, and we did not get sick. Dear daughter, you should have blessed the strange food before you gave it to your child."

Hearing about Sarah's illness, all the Numa came to pray, but she grew steadily worse until her eyes were swollen shut. She had indeed been poisoned, not by the cake, but by touching poison oak, a western shrub something like poison ivy.

Itching, aching, feverish, Sarah lay in bed. When she heard a voice that sounded like an angel, she really thought it was one, for she had been taught that an angel comes to take the soul to the spirit land. Lying so still with her eyes closed, she memorized the angel-words, even though she couldn't understand them.

"Poor little girl, it is too bad!" the angel said.

One day, feeling better, Sarah asked, "What was the angel saying to me?"

At this her mother began to weep because she thought the child was dying, but Sarah exclaimed, "Oh, don't, don't cry! I am getting well—indeed I am. I was only asking what the angel meant by saying," and she carefully repeated the words, " 'Poor little girl, it is too bad!' "

Then her grandfather explained the words and told her that a white woman had made Sarah well by putting medicine on her face.

"Can I see her now?" Sarah asked, for her eyes were open at last.

"Yes, she will come pretty soon. She comes every day," Grandfather replied.

When the lady came and put her white hand on Sarah's forehead, Sarah thought this was, indeed, a beautiful angel. The white people were not all bad, after all! From then on, no longer afraid, she looked forward to each day's visit from the "beautiful angel" who was bringing food and making her well.

As soon as she was able, they moved on, to the ranch of Captain Truckee's friend. During that long, sunny winter, most of the men went up to the mountains to care for the stock, while the women helped with housework. Here Sarah learned to use tables and chairs, and to speak both English and Spanish, because of her quickness at languages.

But the women of her family were unhappy with their men away and pleaded so earnestly with Captain Truckee that he agreed to take them back as soon as the snow was off the mountains. The leave-taking was joyous.

Sarah and her people had to cross this divide when they went
to California. It was lonely and rough, a difficult, terrifying
journey for a timid child riding horseback behind her brother.
AUTHOR

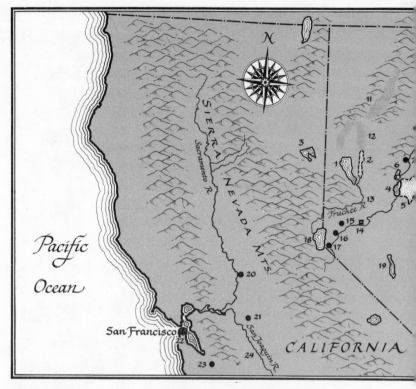

Places of Importance in Sarah's Early Life

1. Pyramid Lake, sacred to the Paiute Indians.
2. Muddy Lake, called Winnemucca Lake today. Site of the Massacre. (now dry)
3. Honey Lake. Chief Winnemucca lived there part of the time.
4. Carson Lake, at lower end of Carson River.
5. Sink of the Carson River
6. Humboldt Lake and Sink. In wet seasons the Humboldt and Carson Sinks sometimes merged into one large lake.
7. Lovelock. Sarah's school was about two miles outside this town.
* 8. Winnemucca. A modern town, named for Chief Winnemucca.
9. Humboldt River, along which thousands of immigrants traveled.
10. Fort McDermitt, where Sarah was interpreter.
11. Black Rock Desert. The Paiutes fled here after the War of 1860.
*12. Smoke Creek Desert.
*13. Truckee River, which flows from Lake Tahoe to Pyramid Lake.

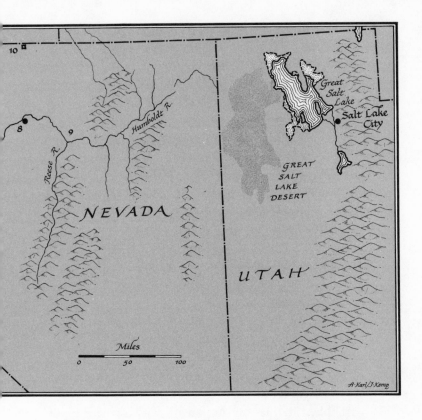

14. Fort Churchill, built after the War of 1860, on Carson River. Sarah and Natchez went there to try to prevent bloodshed.

15. Virginia City, a mining town in the mountains. Sarah lived there at times.

*16. Carson City. Today's capitol of the State of Nevada.

17. Genoa, first called Mormon Station. Sarah lived in Genoa with the Ormsby family.

*18. Lake Tahoe, high in the mountains, in land of the Washoes.

*19. Walker Lake, home of Paiute tribes that were closely allied to those of Pyramid Lake.

20. Sacramento. Sarah and Elma took a steamboat from Sacramento to San Francisco, on their way to school.

21. Stockton, where Sarah fell ill and was healed by the "beautiful angel."

22. San Francisco. Sarah visited Chinatown there on her way to San Jose. Later she often visited and lectured in San Francisco.

23. San Jose, where Sarah and Elma attended the Sisters' school.

24. San Joaquin River. Sarah and her family lived and worked one winter in the valley of this river.

Everybody sang, everybody danced. The women were given dresses. Captain Truckee was paid eight horses for his winter's work, Sarah's brothers received sixteen between them and some money besides, and the other men had two or three horses each—a fortune to the Numa.

Grandpa is right. The settlers are kind, thought Sarah as they rode briskly away. The winter had been a landmark for her, because she had made friends with white people and could speak their language.

But the homecoming wasn't joyous after all. As they were coming down the mountains into the Great Basin, they were met by relatives who wept and said most of the tribe had perished.

"Is my son dead?" Captain Truckee asked, while Sarah held her breath, for he meant her own father, Chief Winnemucca, who had been left in charge.

"No. He has been in the mountains, and those who have been there are all right."

At this, Sarah let out her breath with a great sigh of relief. Her father, in saving his own band from the settlers' guns, had protected them from the mysterious death as well.

The next day, after cutting off their long black hair, they traveled on until they were met by Sarah's father with the rest of the tribe. Although the People had really perished because of a disease, probably cholera, they only knew that one after another would get sick, drink water, and die. Thinking the settlers had poisoned the Humboldt River, they talked wildly of revenge.

However, Captain Truckee was still loyal to his white friends. "My dear children, I am heartily sorry to hear your sad story; but I cannot and will not believe my white brothers would do such a thing," he said, his words tumbling swiftly along. "If they had poisoned the river, they too would have died when they drank of the water. It must be some fearful disease unknown to us. . . .

"You see," he continued, "they are already here in our land; they are all along the river, and we must let our brothers live with us. We cannot tell them to go away. I know your good hearts. I know you won't say *kill them*. Surely you all know that they are human. Their lives are just as dear to them as ours to us."

When at last he finished, Sarah and her mother and sisters embraced Chief Winnemucca, weeping for their dead.

Her grandfather held up his paper. "This is my friend," he said. "Does it look as if it could talk and ask for anything? Yet it can. It can ask for something to eat for me and my people."

Taking Winnemucca with him, he went to the settlement and soon returned with sacks of flour and a new red blanket and shirt for Sarah's father.

She was confused. The whites killed—but they had made her well. They took the Indians' meadows—but gave them horses and presents. They burned stores of food—but they gave food, too.

Would she ever understand these strange people who were overrunning the land?

FOUR

Farewell, Captain Truckee
1852–1859

FOR THE NEXT several years Sarah traveled with her family over the desert. It was beautiful, yet harsh. Sometimes they tried to run from whirling dust clouds that towered hundreds of feet high. After the occasional pounding rainstorms the children could wade gleefully in shallow lakes that might be miles across and six inches deep, but soon dried up, leaving flat, bare valleys called playas.

As the Numa acquired more horses, they met in larger groups and kept in closer touch, with Captain Truckee gaining prestige among both whites and Indians. Steadfastly, he taught Sarah and the People that their only hope lay in friendship with his white brothers, and most settlers who knew the Paiutes well considered them a superior tribe. Early journals and letters called them "good reasoners and thinkers," and "the most intelligent and docile Indians on the continent." They said it was "rare to find a thief among them," and that when trouble occurred, it was generally the fault of the immigrants themselves.

In 1855, when Sarah was about eleven, the Numa and settlers made the treaty of friendship, and the next year Captain Truckee sent Sarah and Elma to the home of Major Ormsby. There Sarah wore long calico dresses and spoke English, seeming almost like a white girl, for as with most Paiutes her skin was not very dark. Round-faced, sparkling, she came to know the settlers and gained experience which later on served her well. But after only a year, when the Washoes were unjustly blamed for the murders, she returned to her family's wandering desert life.

Tensions rose rapidly after 1859, when Sarah was fifteen, for huge amounts of silver were discovered in the Pine Nut Mountains, bringing in miners and adventurers. While the Indians' friends among the settlers tried to keep the treaty, the newcomers neither knew nor cared about it. So many came, destroying the meadows and cutting the pine forests for wood to shore up the mines, that the Indians were hungry. Numaga, the war chief, complained bitterly to his white friends, but they were powerless to help. The bands under Winnemucca and Numaga and most other Paiutes still clung to peace,

The Great Playa, which is more than one hundred miles long. After a heavy rain, it becomes a shallow lake. SESSIONS WHEELER, *The Nevada Desert*

but some began to make raids on the settlements. One government report spoke of the "melancholy picture," said white men occupied most of the good land, and that the Indians were "compelled to either steal or starve." Another said travelers must stop their "infamous practice of shooting them down whenever they happen to see one."

That fall a great sorrow came, for while they were

gathering pine nuts in the mountains, Captain Truckee was bitten by a poisonous snake or insect. The signal fires of death blazed on every mountaintop, and seeing them, the Numa came from far and near, on foot or on horse, to tell their chief farewell. The karnee was crowded with friends and relatives, including a white man named Snyder, whom Truckee had asked for.

The withered, white-haired chief spoke first to Snyder, in a voice scarcely above a whisper. "I am now going to die. I have always loved you as if you were my

dear son; and one thing I want you to do for me." Asking to be raised up, he looked around until he spotted Sarah and Elma.

"You see, there are my two little girls," he said. "I want you to take them to California, to Mr. Bonsal and Mr. Scott. They will send them to school to the sisters, at San Jose. Tell them this is my last request to them." This was a Catholic school, taught by nuns whom Truckee had met in California. Taking Snyder's hand in his own frail, knotted, brown one, he asked, "Will you promise to do this for me?"

When his friend had given his word, Captain Truckee told him goodbye and said, "I want to talk to my own people."

He spoke next to Sarah's father, telling him what he must do in order to be a good father to his family, and a good chief. Exhausted, he slept while the Numa watched and Sarah sat quietly in the dim light, fighting sleep, because she wanted to hear if her grandfather spoke again.

All night and all the next day Captain Truckee slept, until, near midnight, he awoke. "Son, where are you? Come and raise me up," he said, calling for all the children. "I've only a minute to spare. I'm so tired. I

When gold and silver were found in the mountains, miners flocked into Nevada, building shanty towns, throwing refuse and gravel into the streams, and driving out game. They and the settlers changed forever the Indians' way of life. AUTHOR

shall soon be happy. Now, son, I hope you will live to see as much as I have and to know as much as I do. And if you live as I have, you will some day come to me. Do your duty as I have done, to your people and to your white brothers." He paused while the family wept, thinking him dead.

But he opened his eyes once more. "Don't throw away my white rag friend, place it on my breast when you bury me."

"He has spoken his last words," the doctor said. "He has given his last look, his spirit is gone; watch his lips—he will speak as he enters the Spirit-land."

And so it seemed, for his lips moved as if he were whispering.

Long afterward Sarah wrote, "I crept up to him. I could hardly believe he would never speak to me again. I knelt beside him, and took his dear old face in my hands, and looked at him quite a while. I could not speak. I felt the world growing cold; everything seemed dark. The great light had gone out." She thought that if he had put out his hands and asked her to go with him, she would gladly have folded herself in his arms.

Two days later Captain Truckee's body was wrapped in rabbit-skin robes, and his rag friend was placed on his breast as he had asked, to be buried with him. To this day no one knows exactly what Fremont had written on Truckee's cherished paper, but it must have been the highest praise, to serve him so well.

Having visited the missions in California, he had asked for candles to be put at his head and feet, and a

A Paiute *karnee*, similar to the one in which Captain Truckee died, built of willow, cattails, rushes or sagebrush. This is a summer karnee. Those for winter were more tightly constructed and had smoke holes at the top. MARGARET WHEAT

cross to mark his grave, and since the Indians didn't know how to provide these, his white brothers helped them. All felt that a great man had gone, a man who had been a friend to both settlers and Indians, a man who would be needed in the hard days to come.

Sarah, grieving, missed her grandfather and felt that no one could take his place. She never forgot his teachings, but built her life on his belief that the Paiutes' only hope of safety lay in friendship with the white man.

FIVE

War!
1860

THAT WAS such a winter as Sarah had never seen
before. Day after day after day the temperature
was below freezing, snow was heaped in drifts, and
supplies of stored food were small. When only Indians
had lived on the land, they could find all they needed,
but now that the white men had destroyed so much of
the game and grass and pine nuts, they weren't ready
for such terrible cold. Isaac Roop, a leading man among
the settlers, said the natives were freezing and starving
by scores, and that in one home he had found three dead
or dying children. Although the government sent some
supplies, they weren't enough. Many Indians blamed
the immigrants for all their troubles, and when settlers
offered food, they refused because they feared it was

poisoned. Hungry, wrapped in all their robes, Sarah and her family and friends huddled miserably in their karnees, waiting for spring.

When it came at last, melting the snow and opening the pass, Sarah and Elma set off for California, escorted by Natchez and five other warriors. It was a grueling trip. At the head of Carson River they had to walk for more than two miles through a canyon, while the stage pitched and rolled among rocks half its size. In the mountains part of the road was so steep that they again had to walk, often through knee-deep dust. They probably camped at night, because the primitive inns wouldn't admit Indians.

Sarah was interested in everything. She saw a Pony Express rider on his panting horse, rode a steamboat down the Sacramento River, visited a fish market, and strolled through Chinatown, where she pitied the pig-tailed women hobbling on their tiny feet.

After the stop in San Francisco, Captain Truckee's friend, Mr. Scott, took the two girls to the Sisters of Notre Dame School at San Jose, housed in a splendid brick building. This was a new school, founded by Belgian nuns who taught grammar, history, geography, arithmetic, needlework and music—along with philosophy, mythology, and "epistology" (letter-writing). They gave large gold medals or silk and velvet crowns for "mending" and "lady-like deportment."

There Sarah and Elma filed into the dining room to eat with forks and spoons, sat on benches for classes, and slept in clean, white-curtained beds in the upstairs dorm-

San Jose in 1857, just before Sarah went there to attend the Convent School of Notre Dame. It is the building with the steeple at the extreme right of the picture. CALIFORNIA STATE LIBRARY

itory. Sixteen-year-old Sarah, developing a passionate interest in needlework, spent happy hours with her glossy black head bent over the bright-colored threads. Just outside the mission walls flowed a canal in which Mexican women washed clothes, and beyond that stretched the desert, blooming with yellow flowers of wild mustard. Inside, all was peace and beauty, with lawns and flower beds, poplars and palms. Sarah loved the school and joyously crammed her mind with every possible scrap of learning.

But well-to-do Spanish-speaking parents of some students objected to having their children associate with Indians, and the school couldn't exist without their support. After only three weeks, the nuns called Sarah and Elma aside to explain, sadly, and as gently as possible, that they must leave.

Heavy-hearted, the two girls walked for the last time through the gate. Since Natchez couldn't come for them, Mr. Scott put them on the stagecoach, to make their way alone back to the Great Basin. Brief as it was, this had been a very important experience for Sarah, who had now attended a real school and knew what classes and teachers, lessons and routines, were like.

When she reached Pyramid Lake, she found that the smoldering Indian resentment had burst into a blaze of anger, and a great gathering of Paiutes ready for war had come to the lake. The chief from Powder River was there, chiefs from Smoke Creek, Honey Lake, the Humboldt Meadows, Black Rock Desert, and dozens of others. Sarah could see their campfires flickering.

She didn't take part in the councils, for her time as leader hadn't yet come. Instead, she was probably one of the women who gathered roots of marsh plants and eggs of the birds that nested there by thousands, or cleaned *cui-ui*, the big, ugly, delicious fish of Pyramid Lake. While the women worked, the solemn chiefs in their circle by the fire were making a grave decision.

Five times they sent the pipe around. Although the Indians had faithfully kept the treaty, many of the whites had not. An old Paiute man, hunting rabbits, had been bound and dragged until he had no skin on his bones. A chief's son had been slain. Men had been murdered, women seized, until all patience was at an end. Even Winnemucca was known to favor war, although he didn't openly urge it. Of all the chiefs only one—Sarah's cousin Numaga, the War Chief—spoke out for peace.

Six feet tall, broad-chested, with keen, unflinching black eyes, Numaga was especially admired by settlers, who called him "not just a superior Indian but a superior man of any race." Numaga rode from camp to camp, beseeching the People not to fight a war that could only end in disaster. When they met him with calm silence,

Pages following

A typical stagecoach of the 1850s traveling through the California mountains. Sarah and Elma crossed the Sierra Nevada Mountains by stagecoach when they returned from the Sisters' School at San Jose. WELLS FARGO BANK HISTORY ROOM, SAN FRANCISCO

Numaga, the heroic Paiute chief who led the combined tribes in the Pyramid Lake War. Although he was a warrior, he steadfastly worked for peace and friendship with the whites.
AUTHOR

he lay face down on the ground and fasted for three days, motionless, brooding. He was so earnest that men began to swing to his support, and this angered their leaders. Sarah's father said in scorn, "Your skin is red, but your heart is white; go away and live among the palefaces." Others threatened to kill him.

At last Numaga stood up and spoke for an hour. "The white men are like the stars over your heads. You have wrongs, great wrongs that rise up like those mountains before you; but can you, from the mountaintops, reach and blot out those stars? Your enemies are like the sands in the bed of your rivers . . . They will come like the sand in a whirlwind and drive you from your homes."

Just as he had nearly won the chiefs over, a messenger galloped in on a foam-flecked pony and gasped out fearful news. Several warriors, including Sarah's brother Natchez, had slipped away from camp to look for two lost Paiute girls and had found them held prisoner beneath the floor of a barn. When they released the girls and saw their condition, the warriors were so overcome by anger that they burned the barn and killed several white men, including its owner.

When the messenger finished, Numaga's deep voice broke the silence. "There is no longer any use for counsel. We must prepare for war, for the soldiers will now come here to fight us."

The long peace between Sarah's people and the white man was over.

She herself didn't go into battle. Not yet. Instead, she and the other women and children stayed behind the

Black Rock Desert, the forbidding land of mountains and
canyons where Numaga led the People after their defeat.
SESSIONS WHEELER, *The Black Rock Desert*

warriors while a volunteer army marched out from the
settlements, led by her friend, Major Ormsby.

Recklessly, the volunteers came down the Truckee
River, almost to Pyramid Lake, where Numaga had
taken command as War Chief. First, he offered a truce.

It was refused. Next, he lured the army down the steep river banks into a trap. And even then, when the whites began to retreat, he rushed ahead, waved back his warriors, and tried to obtain a parley. But year after year the Indians had suppressed so much rage that now they were out of Numaga's control. Yelling, they dashed by him, pursued the army, and slaughtered most of it, including Major Ormsby.

So the major, Sarah's friend, was slain by her own people—who were fighting for their very existence. Again she was torn two ways. However, she had little time to mourn, for professional soldiers in smart blue uniforms marched over the mountains from California, and the women and children fled toward the north. No matter how great Numaga's skill, his warriors were no match for this strong new force. He managed to protect the women as they escaped, but he lost the battle, and with it the war.

Sarah undoubtedly fled with the Numa, floundering in deep snow over the mountains to the fearsome Black Rock Desert, a great flat white alkali plain surrounded by jagged cliffs and dark, winding canyons that were easy to defend. It was treeless, cold at night, with no daytime shelter from the shimmering sun. Worse, it offered little food and water, while pitiless storms howled in and stifling dust blew like "billows of foam." Sarah, however, escaped some of the hardships. With the fighting over and Numaga still serving as chief, Winnemucca was no longer needed in Nevada, so he took his family to distant Paiute tribes in Oregon.

Although the Numa longed for their lakes and rivers, the soldiers were building a "hiding place" of adobe and stone—Fort Churchill—on the Carson River, and that made it dangerous to return. Neither side wished to continue the fight, for the settlers wanted an end to Indian attacks, and the Indians were tired of hiding in the rocks, and were hungry.

Meeting the army officers, Numaga bitterly told

them that white men had received more than they had given, that they were "like coyotes, always ready to eat and to bark. They make a heap of talk and much of their talk is not good." But he pledged the Paiutes not to make war for a year, provided the white men also kept the peace.

This was too important an agreement to make without Winnemucca, the "head chief," so the Paiutes sent for him. Back Sarah came with her father, and at a meeting in the desert the Indians formally promised to lay down their arms in return for protection and a reservation—a piece of their own land including both Pyramid and Muddy Lakes. They were also to receive food, supplies, teachers and help in learning to farm. Along with many of her family, Sarah prepared to settle down to reservation life.

Even by the white man's rules her people now owned their beloved Pyramid Lake. But never again would the whole, windy, colorful Great Basin be freely theirs.

SIX

End of Freedom
1860–1866

WITH THE WAR OVER and a reservation established, things seemed brighter, but for both Sarah and her people heartbreak was ahead. For a while she lived at Pyramid Lake, where the agent was big, handsome, kindly Warren Wasson, called "Long Beard" by the Indians. Wasson encouraged the Numa to dig a ditch for a mill, helped them farm the few acres of good crop land, nagged the government for supplies, and when medicine didn't come, he furnished it himself. One day when he was issuing hickory shirts, blue overalls and calico, a very old man was desolate because he arrived after everything was gone. "Long Beard" didn't hesitate. To the People's delight, he peeled off his own shirt and "drawers" (trousers) and handed them over.

Other Indians, living off the reservation, suffered that winter, which, again, was bitterly cold. Wasson reported half-starved tribesmen hanging around the stage coach stations, living on "the undigested barley obtained by washing the manure from the Overland Stables in baskets, after the manner of separating gold from earth with a pan."

Warren Wasson was the kindly agent at the newly formed Pyramid Lake Reservation. NEVADA STATE MUSEUM

For Sarah, this was the beginning of several restless years. She often traveled from tribe to tribe with her father, who was urging his followers to keep the peace, and she always enjoyed being with her people, sitting on the ground, joining their gambling games, and sharing their pine nut mush and pollen cakes.

The Paiutes were still a loose confederacy of small bands, each with its own leader but Winnemucca was their "head chief." Tall, with a deeply lined face, he appeared ferocious because of the four-inch bone he wore in his nose, although he was actually mild. Sometimes he put on a feather headdress, rode into a settlement, and made a street-corner speech, while Sarah interpreted and two braves held a red and white crescent above his head. When a great "peace talk" was held on the reservation, he swooped in with four hundred warriors who performed a continuous war dance for two days, part of it on live coals.

In 1861, the first year of the Civil War, Nevada was separated from Utah and became a territory, and the next year "Long Beard" left the agency. Since she had relatives at Pyramid Lake, Sarah now received a disheartening glimpse of what an agent could be, for the ones after Wasson were either incompetent, or rascals, or both. Some were kindly but weak. Others sold government supplies to line their own pockets, and let white squatters take the best land, seize timber, cut hay, steal cattle, and fish in Pyramid Lake. One recommended reducing the reservation from six hundred square miles to forty. Another had a large strip turned over to the railroad, which was just being built. In addition, the government appropriated so little money that the "good" agents must constantly plead for more food, more clothing, more medicine. One said he could issue "only flour and not enough of that," and another reported fifteen hundred people "almost totally without food."

Bitterly resentful, restless, homeless, Sarah sometimes lived in the settlements instead of with her father, and she was briefly married to an Indian, whom she said she divorced for his "extreme cruelty." We don't know whether the marriage and divorce were according to the white man's laws, or those of the Numa.

Moving to the Indian shanty town at the edge of Virginia City, in the Pine Nut Mountains, she saw all too clearly how her people suffered. Paiute women crept out before dawn, carrying baskets into which they eagerly dropped stray wisps of hay, half-rotten fruit, wilted carrots, heads and tails of fish from the refuse dumps. Occasionally a kind-hearted citizen would give them a sack of flour or a bowl of leavings from the slaughterhouse. Often when the shift came out of the mines, Indian women and children would be waiting in line, holding out baskets into which the miners would empty leftover food from their lunch pails.

Sarah herself trudged from door to door, peddling the needlework she had learned at the sisters' school, and whenever she got together a little money, she amazed the miners by buying grammar and history books. Now in her late teens, vivacious, outspoken, she had an old-gold complexion, fashionably curled hair, and

Virginia City in 1859, in the Paiute's Pine Nut Mountains.
The miners cut acres of pine nut trees to build this city and
shore up the mines, which honeycombed the ground it stood
on. Sarah lived here off and on for several years. THE

the ability to speak English and Spanish, to read and write. Newspaper stories, which called her "Princess Sarah," said she often filled out a square at a miners' dance while a "yaller-backed fiddle" played the tunes.

The earliest known picture of Sarah, drawn while she was living in Virginia City after the Pyramid Lake War. AUTHOR

By the end of the Civil War in 1865, Nevada had become a state instead of a territory. That fall some Indians in the north were accused of stealing cattle, and an army set out from Fort Churchill, the "hiding place," to arrest them. However, instead of marching north the soldiers stopped at Muddy Lake on the reservation. Sarah's sister Elma was there, and later on, in her book, Sarah repeated Elma's story.

"Oh, dear readers, these soldiers had gone only sixty miles away to Muddy Lake, where my people were then living and fishing, and doing nothing to anyone. The soldiers rode up to their encampment and fired into it, and killed almost all the people that were there . . . It was all old men, women and children that were killed; for my father had all the young men with him, at the sink of Carson on a hunting excursion, or they would have been killed too. After the soldiers had killed all but some little children and babies still tied up in their baskets, the soldiers took them also, and set the camp on fire and threw them into the flames to see them burn alive. I had one baby brother killed there. My sister jumped on father's best horse and ran away. As she ran, the soldiers ran after her; but, thanks be to the Good Father in the Spirit-land, my dear sister got away."

Other Indians, including Numaga, said two of the slain women were Winnemucca's wives.

When the white people heard what had happened, many of them, the fair-minded ones, were incensed. Although the army insisted it had fought a battle against warriors, newspaper editors asked why no prisoners or

Chief Winnemucca wearing a feather crown, as he appeared on his visits to Virginia City. NEVADA STATE HISTORICAL SOCIETY

weapons had been taken, and why—as the army ad- mitted—women had been killed. An investigation was demanded, but never made.

Before the outcry had fully quieted down, an Indian wandered into a supply station, where a white man per- suaded him to look into the barrel of his gun, then pulled the trigger. A few days later the victim's tribe pounced on the station and wiped out all its occupants. These two events, the "Muddy Lake Massacre" and the raid on the station, set off ten months of war, a conflict that Sarah sadly called "the trail which is marked by the blood of my people from hill to hill and from valley to valley."

By the time it was over, her family was crumbling. Her mother and older sister Mary had both died. Heart- broken, Chief Winnemucca was spending most of his time with distant Paiute tribes in Oregon. Her sister Elma had gone to Montana, married a white rancher, and turned her back on Indian life.

Although lively Sarah could also have moved into the white world, she had seen enough of "civilization." Packing her precious books, she traveled down the moun- tain, away from Virginia City, to Pyramid Lake, where her older brother Natchez was living.

And there Sarah Winnemucca, daughter of a chief, became a leader in her own right.

SEVEN

Riding
in the Night
1866–1867

SARAH SOON FOUND that the reservation was not run by a kindly agent such as Warren Wasson, but by a man named Nugent, who disliked the People and gave them so little they sometimes hadn't a scrap to eat. Even so, she and her sister-in-law, Natchez's wife, were luckier than many, for they washed clothes for the agent's family, and were generally paid a little flour.

Nugent had no scruples. Although supplying the Indians with gunpowder was illegal, he sold some to a Paiute, and when one of his aides discovered the powder he promptly shot the unfortunate brave. Muttering wild threats of revenge, the People then began to gather, and

Sarah, who still believed with all her heart in Captain Truckee's teachings, urged Natchez to warn the agent. Hurriedly, they saddled their horses and galloped away in the dark.

It was a wild ride. The river, which they had to cross, was high. Sarah's horse fell in midstream. She was swept off his back to flounder in the muddy water. Realizing what had happened, Natchez jumped off his own horse—groped—found her—helped her back on. And dripping wet, they rode to the agency.

"Mr. Nugent, go away! Quick!" Sarah cried. "My people are coming here to kill you. Tell all who live by the river to go too, for they will surely come and kill them all."

Nugent didn't share her horror of bloodshed. "I am not afraid of them—we have a good many guns," he replied, and called to his men, "Get your guns ready; we will show the damned red devils how to fight."

"We would like to have you go; please do not get us into any more trouble," pleaded Natchez.

But Nugent didn't agree, or thank them for warning him, or offer them a meal and shelter, although he must have seen how wet and cold they were. "Go away," he curtly said.

Pages following

Fort Churchill, the "hiding place," which the army built on the Carson River to control the Paiutes. Sarah and Natchez rode to this fort in their attempt to prevent trouble. NEVADA STATE MUSEUM

Dispirited, Sarah and Natchez returned home, where they called the Numa together, explained the danger, and sent ten young men to watch the river crossing, in case anyone tried to get through. They were to shoot their own people, if necessary. "We must do it, or we will all be in trouble," Natchez cautioned them, for he and Sarah knew that even one white death might bring many to the Indians. He then left, to keep watch.

In spite of the sentinels, during that dark night some of the angry Numa managed to reach the agency, found Nugent away, killed one of his men and wounded another. When the agent returned and discovered what had happened, he went straight to the army at Fort Churchill.

Since Sarah was the only Paiute with an education, the captain of the fort wrote her a letter and sent it by two warriors.

"Miss Sarah Winnemucca,

Your agent tells us very bad things about your people's killing two of our men. I want you and your brother Natchez to meet me at your place tonight. I want to talk to you and your brother.

Signed,
CAPTAIN JEROME
Company M, 8th Cavalry.

With Sarah's brief schooling, it wasn't easy for her to read handwriting, but she puzzled over it until she knew what it said. As the exciting news spread from house to house her friends gathered, begging her to tell them the news.

"The soldiers are coming," Sarah said. "The officer wants me and my brother to see them at our place."

The People thought she should reply. "Can you speak to them on paper?" they asked.

Sarah hesitated. "I have nothing to write with. I have no ink. I have no pen."

"Oh, take a stick—take anything!" they cried. "Until you talk on that paper we will not believe you can."

Sarah thought for a moment. The soldiers would be disappointed if they came and Natchez was still away. Should she ask them to wait at the fort? Quickly she formed a plan. "Make me a stick with a sharp point, and bring me some fish's blood," she said. When they were brought, she wrote, with many pauses to dip the stick,

"Hon. Sir,
My brother is not here. I am looking for him every minute. We will go as soon as he comes in. If he comes tonight, we will come some time during the night.
Yours,
S.W.

Hours dragged by. When at last Natchez returned, he and Sarah set out, riding like the wind, never stopping, going this time not to the agency but all the way to Fort Churchill.

Paiutes at Pyramid Lake, photographed about 1867. Sarah
undoubtedly knew most of these people, and the man near

the center, in profile, with the high forehead, is thought
to be Natchez. TIMOTHY O'SULLIVAN

The agent, Nugent, who was already there, watched with cold eyes while Sarah talked with the officer, but she didn't falter. In a torrent of words she told Captain Jerome everything from the beginning of trouble—that the agent himself had sold the powder, that the agent's own man had killed the Indian, that her people were starving, that the agent failed to give them the food and clothing that the government provided. She told how she and Natchez had taken Nugent a warning, and how rudely he had replied. Without a word in his own defense, the agent listened as Sarah talked on and on.

The captain was interested, for more than a hundred hollow-cheeked, starving Paiutes had come to his fort the summer before. He asked Sarah and Natchez many questions and invited them to stay at the fort overnight. But Sarah insisted on returning to their People, to tell them the army was coming.

In the morning, true to his word, the officer appeared at the reservation, and camped there. When he inquired about their food and learned they truly had nothing to eat, he sent for three wagonloads of provisions.

"If you want to issue beef to the Indians, I have some cattle I can sell you," suggested the agent. But the officer, disgusted, told him to "be off," because these were the very cattle the government had sent for free gifts to the Indians.

Five days later other soldiers brought a letter that asked where Chief Winnemucca was. Weeping, Sarah told the messenger that her father had not been in since her little brother was killed at Muddy Lake, but had sent word he was going to live in the mountains and die there.

"Sarah, don't cry," the officer said. "The commanding officer says you are to go with me to Camp McDermitt, and you can get your father and all your people to come into the army post, where you can be fed."

Camp McDermitt was much farther north, close to the Oregon boundary, but still in the Great Basin. If Sarah and Natchez and their people went there, they would leave Pyramid Lake, the Pine Nut Mountains, the springs and marshes they knew and loved. Some were afraid, but others were willing. As Natchez said, "Because some white people are bad that is no reason why the soldiers should be bad too."

So they told the captain they would go.

EIGHT

The Black-Clothes Fathers
1867–1874

ON A HOT DAY in early July Sarah and Natchez started north with Company M, First Cavalry, amid a din of hoofs, wheels, shouts and bugles. For nearly a month they jogged along on tough little horses, sweltering under the sun, for the trip was three hundred dusty miles. At last, almost at the Oregon border, they plodded out of a mountain pass into the flat valley where the stone buildings of Fort McDermitt stood. At headquarters, cool and shaded by a long verandah, Sarah was given a room of her own.

Their first morning at the fort the commanding officer, Major Dudley Seward, sent for Sarah and Natchez. "Do you think you can find your father?" he asked, explaining that white settlers were so angry at Indian raids that the army was going to hunt down all who were not on reservations. "I am afraid to have your father out there. Natchez, if you can bring him in, I will feed him and his people, and will give them clothes such as the soldiers wear. I will be his friend and fight for him if he and his people are good."

Sarah was not one to stand quietly and listen. Thinking of her people's early, happy life, and their recent misery, thinking of her father, a chief, who must come meekly in and "be good," like a little boy, she broke out, "Colonel, my papa has never done anything unkind to the white people yet, and the soldiers came to Muddy Lake and killed a great many of our people. . . . They killed my little brother. This is what drove my poor papa away. We have not seen him for two years."

Even though Sarah was so eloquent, the colonel didn't yet know how capable she was, so he chose Natchez to go for Winnemucca. In a few days, he returned with nearly five hundred Paiutes, who were given a place to camp, rations, and castoff uniforms. Always emotional, Sarah embraced her father with tears of joy.

Since she spoke five languages—English, Spanish, Paiute, Washoe and Shoshone—she was hired as interpreter at sixty-five dollars per month, and one day the commanding officer called her in.

"How many companies of soldiers would it take, Sarah, to escort the Paiutes from C. F. Smith here?" he asked, referring to a tribe who were living in extreme poverty about sixty miles away.

Sarah dressed like a white girl, as she appeared while she lived at Fort McDermitt. NEVADA HISTORICAL SOCIETY

"None," she replied. "You and I could escort them, or Lee and I." Lee was her younger brother, a tall, handsome boy in his teens, who had come in with Winnemucca.

At first the colonel couldn't believe that a young woman and a boy could lead a whole band of people, but Sarah was so emphatic that he finally let her and Lee set out alone, jogging across the sagebrush desert under the summer sun.

At the Indians' camp, Sarah sat around the council fire one whole weary night, trying to persuade them to come. At last she convinced them that the army was kind, and soon she was proudly riding beside Lee at the head of four hundred Paiutes. Bright-eyed babies gazed solemnly from their cradle-boards, bent old women leaned on sticks and carried all their possessions in baskets on their backs.

Now nine hundred Indians lived at Camp McDermitt. Every morning at five o'clock the women came, each with her number on a tag fastened to a leather thong around her neck. Clutching a basket, the woman told the size of her family and what she needed, and twenty-three-year-old Sarah issued rations for the day—a pound and a half of meat and good bread for every adult, with coffee, sugar, salt, pepper and beans once a month. The grateful Numa called the soldiers their "black-clothes fathers."

For the next three years Sarah lived happily at Fort McDermitt, where her people looked up to her and trusted her. She prevented at least one serious outbreak

Fort McDermitt, where Sarah served as interpreter. NEVADA
HISTORICAL SOCIETY

when a man named Joe Lindsey shot and scalped an
Indian, infuriating the Paiutes to the verge of war. Sarah
reminded them of the teachings of Captain Truckee and
talked for hours until they returned quietly to their
camp.

She dressed like a white woman, one outfit being a
tight-fitting black suit trimmed with green fringe. With
her excellent English, smooth skin and flashing dark
eyes, she was attractive to the young officers, and doubtless she found them glamorous, joked with them, and
rode with them—side-saddle like a white girl—across the
valley.

But the happy times couldn't last. In 1869, President Grant named a board of Indian commissioners, who adopted a new policy. Instead of making treaties with the tribes as nations, the federal government now considered the Indians as its wards and required them to leave the army camps and go to reservations.

This set off a squabble between the army and the Bureau of Indian Affairs, a squabble that soon involved Sarah. The Bureau wanted to turn the Indians into "civilized" farmers. The army thought the best way to keep them peaceful was to let them follow their own customs and feed them well. The Bureau said the army spoiled the red men. The army issued biting reports of starving natives who came to the forts for help. While many of the Indian agents were cruel, the real trouble was caused by callous policy makers in Washington. One official report blandly said the Washoes had no reservation, but were dying off so fast that "none is required." It was a national scandal that men of the "Indian ring" were fattening their own wallets with money that had been appropriated to help the Indians.

Sarah—brainy, fiery, tough—got into the scrap by acting as interpreter for Major Henry Douglass, who came to Fort McDermitt to explain the plans for moving them to reservations.

One chief vowed he would never consent. "I was taken to the reservation three years ago," he said. "We had nothing to live on. Measles got among us—many suffered and died. There is no game on the reservation. . . . If I had nothing and my back was blistering in the hot sun I would stay here. Do not ask me to leave. . . .

I will stay here and lay my bones here with my dead children."

One was ironic. "If any white people see any of my people out on the hills digging for roots don't say we are on the war path."

Others spoke of an Indian killed by a Justice of the Peace, of five murdered while on their way to the fort. As she interpreted, Sarah became so upset she burst into angry words of her own.

"White men kill Indians and all right—nothing is done with them, they are not hanged nor hurt at all—not so with Indians—they kill white man and they are killed right off."

Some of her people wanted to fight. Some fled into the hills. A few, including Sarah, stayed stubbornly on at the fort. Numaga, the gallant chief who had led the Paiutes in the Pyramid Lake War, was unable to guide them now, because he was desperately ill with a white man's disease—tuberculosis—which soon took his life.

Determined to help her people and in a fury at their treatment, Sarah wrote a letter in amazingly good English, describing their hardships, and sent it to the Major Douglass who had just visited the fort. With this letter she entered the national scene, because he forwarded it to the Commissioner of Indian Affairs.

Before long she wrote again, and still again, and officials began to know her name. If her people were forced onto reservations, she said, settlers would suffer, and Indians would suffer even more.

"I being Chief Winnemucca's daughter they look

to me for help," she wrote. "Many being on the borders of starvation, have left their houses and wandered we know not where . . . we would all much rather be slain and put out of our misery than to be lingering here— each day bringing new sorrows—and finally to die of hunger and starvation."

But not all was trouble, for Sarah fell in love with a dashing young officer, Lieutenant Edward Bartlett. True to her nature, she overcame all obstacles and recklessly ignored advice, even from her family. No matter that her father and brothers had heard Bartlett was a drunkard. Sarah was determined. No matter that Nevada law forbade marriage between Indians and whites. Sarah found a way. In January, 1871, she eloped with her lieutenant to Salt Lake City and spent a brief honeymoon there.

However, all too soon she realized how right her family had been, for Bartlett's carousing was too much to endure. Before the year was out, she separated from him, and as soon as she scraped together enough money, she got a divorce.

In spite of her personal trouble, when her people asked her to go to San Francisco and tell the commanding general about their plight, she promptly put on her best clothes and started out. She may have gone by train, because the Central Pacific Railroad was complete by now, and Indians were allowed to ride free.

This trip, to speak to the highest officials she could find, marked another giant step in her development. San Franciscans were fascinated by the fiery young Indian princess, and newspapers printed admiring stories about

Interior of a parlor car of the Central Pacific, the railroad that passed through Pyramid Lake Reservation. Indians were allowed to ride the freight cars of this line free, but the Winnemucca family could travel in the passenger coaches. Sarah rode the Central Pacific many times. AUTHOR

her. However, the general merely sent her to Nevada to see a senator—who gave her twenty dollars and promises he didn't keep. Sarah then went right back to San Francisco, where she again received publicity but no help. Returning to Nevada empty-handed, she joined her father's wandering band.

She wasn't silent long. The next year Winnemucca galloped into Fort McDermitt, bringing Sarah and about sixty followers. While she interpreted, he bitterly reminded the officers that the Indians had been promised food and clothing if they remained peaceful, that he had never broken his word, but agents had. Now, he said, he had only two choices: to starve, or to steal cattle and be shot by the soldiers.

Again Sarah spoke out, saying that if her people weren't helped they would have to rebel—and she would join them. "I am quite willing to throw off the garments of civilization I now wear," she said, "and mount my pony. I well remember the time when the hills surrounding this very camp were swarming with hostile Indians, and then the officers talked very sweetly to me."

Much as they wanted to help, the soldiers were powerless to do anything for the Indians, because the government forbade it. Grieving, Winnemucca turned away, to lead a fragment of his once happy tribe from valley to valley. Grieving, yet rejecting the life of a wanderer, Sarah watched him go.

Her army friends couldn't help her. Her father was homeless, her marriage destroyed, her tribe scattered.

Sarah was adrift.

NINE

Two Agents of Malheur
1875–1877

THE NEXT MAY, 1875, while Sarah was visiting Winnemucca's camp, her young brother Lee rode breathlessly in from the brand new Malheur Reservation in Oregon. He brought a letter offering Sarah a job as interpreter at forty dollars a month, and when her father agreed to go with her, she, Winnemucca and Lee set out briskly, making the trip in a single day. Within a few months her father left, but Sarah stayed on.

At Malheur she found another agent to admire —patient, honest Sam Parrish, whom she followed around, interpreting, as he showed the Indians what to do. "The reservation is all yours. The government has given it to you and your children," he said.

Sam Parrish, agent at Malheur Reservation, and one of the few agents Sarah admired. OREGON HISTORICAL SOCIETY

For all his kindness, he was firm, and told them, "I have no time to throw away. I have come to show you how to work, and work we must." Besides having them dig an irrigation ditch, cut rails for fences, and sow crops, he promised to train three young men as blacksmiths and three as carpenters, and had them begin building a school where Sarah was to teach.

All summer, while the tribe worked with a will, Parrish fed them well, and in the fall when the harvest was in, he gave the men powder and lead for the hunt.

"Oh, how happy my people were!" Sarah wrote. "That night we all got together and had a dance."

When the hunters returned, Mr. Parrish made a wonderful issue—ten yards of calico for every woman, plus flannel, muslin and shawls; pantaloon goods, handkerchiefs, shoes, stockings for the boys; blankets, shirts, pants, hats, looking glasses and shoes for the men. Only two were empty-handed: Sarah, because she received a salary; and little, ugly, quick-witted Chief Oytes, half-Bannock and half-Paiute, who had refused to work. Most of the Paiutes were afraid of Oytes, who claimed his magic could kill them all, and boasted that no bullets could harm him. He was furious he had received no gifts.

Since Sarah was interpreter, the Paiutes looked up to her, and that night they came running. "Oytes is coming over to kill the agent!" they cried. "We have said everything to him. We have given him our blankets, but that isn't enough. What will we do?"

"We will tell Mr. Parrish," Sarah promptly replied, and hurried away.

The next morning Mr. Parrish sent for the chief. "Oytes," he said, touching his gun, "I have three hundred dollars. If you will let me shoot at you, if my bolt won't go through your body, the money is yours. You say bolts cannot kill you." He raised his gun.

"Oh, my good father, don't kill me!" Oytes cried out, sagging in terror.

"All right, Oytes; don't let me hear any more of your talk."

"No, good father, I will not say anything more."

They shook hands, after which Parrish gave Oytes a red blanket, shirts, hat, pants and shoes.

It was a happy winter. Sarah and Mrs. Parrish held classes in the new school for Paiute children, who came shyly, fascinated by the clock, colored pictures and maps. Often, while they recited and sang, Indian women gathered outside the open windows to listen. One of the best pupils was Mattie, gentle, kindhearted, with long, shining hair and a slow soft voice like songs. To Sarah's delight, her brother Lee fell in love with Mattie and married her.

When spring tinged the bare hills with green, General O. O. Howard, commanding officer for the whole area, came to visit Malheur, bringing his young daughter. Howard, who had lost his right arm in the Civil War, was a kindly man and especially interested in Indians. Sarah helped make him and his daughter comfortable, and that night, when a noisy Indian dance alarmed them, she assured them it was only to celebrate their visit. This began a long friendship.

General Oliver O. Howard, who became Sarah's friend when he visited Malheur Reservation. Later, Sarah was his trusted scout and interpreter during the Bannock War. AUTHOR

That same spring the Paiutes were overjoyed because Mr. Parrish assigned them individual plots of ground, which they proudly began to plant. But the settlers, who could never stop coveting Indian land, sent a petition to Washington, which demanded the west end of the reservation and accused the Indians of not working. Ridiculous though the charge was, as shown by the irrigation ditch, fenced fields, the crops, school and other buildings, the Indians had no friend in Washington to help them.

A worse blow soon fell, for Parrish called everyone to the school house and told them he must leave. "The man who is coming here to take care of you is a good man," he said. "You must do just as he wants you to."

Reckless Chief Oytes jumped up. "We will not let our father go! We will fight for him . . . I want some of the young men to go and tell Winnemucca to come here as soon as he can."

"Yes, send for Winnemucca," the others agreed.

It was no use, even though Sarah's father came and, with her to interpret, led a delegation of protest to Camp Harney. The new agent, Rinehart, was a local storekeeper with citizens' backing. He received the post.

In July, when Rinehart arrived, Sarah went along as Mr. Parrish pointed out the plots of ground, planted and sprouting and marked with the Indian owners' names. She heard him praise the Paiutes' honesty and willingness to work and explain that they had not yet received the year's issue. Rinehart listened, seeming to agree.

However, as soon as he was left in charge, he began

to give Indian goods to his own family and friends. He told the Paiutes he would pay them for working, but when they gathered on payday to receive their money and goods, he merely issued credit, then charged so much for the past week's food that they had very little left.

One of the assembled chiefs was Egan, Mattie's uncle, a burly, handsome, short-haired fellow, quite young, and an expert fisherman and mountain climber. Chief Egan jumped to his feet.

"Why do you want to play with us?" he demanded. "We are men, not children. We want our father to deal with us like men and tell us just what he wants us to do, but don't say you are going to pay us money and then not do it." He asked for the cash they had earned.

"I will give you an order on a store in Canyon City," offered Rinehart.

Egan was disgusted. "Our good father Sam Parrish sent for these things which are in the store for us, and you want us to pay for them. You are all wearing the clothes that we fools thought belonged to us." Turning toward his men, he ordered them to go home, at which the agent flew into a rage and told them all to leave.

That night the angry Paiutes called Sarah to their council fire. Rinehart was dishonest, they said. They had been patient long enough and wanted to go to the soldiers again. But she persuaded them to wait.

Nothing improved. Later, in speeches and in her book, Sarah was to cite Rinehart as an example of all that was worst in the Bureau of Indian Affairs. She said that when a few Paiutes from Pyramid Lake arrived on a

Sunday, tired and hungry, Rinehart wouldn't let her give them rations because it was the Lord's Day. When he thought, mistakenly, that a small Indian boy was laughing at him, he picked up the child by his ear and threw him onto the ground, severely injuring him. When a frightened boy seemed impudent, he had him handcuffed and threatened a hanging.

Rinehart's own reports confirmed much of this. Like most agents, he tried to picture himself as honest and kindhearted, but over and again he revealed his true nature. He admitted that he paid the Indians only half of what they could earn by working for settlers. He acknowledged the handcuffing, expressed profound scorn for the Paiutes, called them lazy and disrespectful, and said their children should be taken away from their "wild and debasing influence."

The problems were not entirely Rinehart's fault, for like other agents he was struggling with skimpy funds. Newspapers, army reports and letters of outraged citizens repeatedly protested that the Paiutes were starving, and E. A. Hoyt himself, Commissioner of Indian Affairs, said they couldn't exist on the supplies allowed.

Rinehart insisted that Parrish had managed to appear generous only by running up a huge debt, and that funds were steadily being cut—from $50,000 to $40,000 —to $25,000—to $20,000. He complained that the Indians' total support per person was only five cents a day, and that goods were eleven months coming, leaving the rest of the year to be run "on faith and credit." Rinehart was cruel, but so was the system.

This early cartoon was entitled "Savages!" It expresses the
outrage many white people felt for the cruelty with which the
Paiutes were treated.

One morning, when Chiefs Egan and Oytes with all their men came to say their children were dying of hunger, and Rinehart again refused to help them, Egan folded his arms across his broad chest and commanded Sarah, "I want you to tell everything I say to this man."

She drew a deep breath.

"Did the government tell you to come here and drive us off this reservation?" Egan began. "Did the Big Father say, go and kill us all off, so you can have our land? Did he tell you to pull our children's ears off, and put handcuffs on them, or carry a pistol to shoot us with?" He paused for Sarah to interpret. "We want to know how the government came by this land. Is the government mightier than our Spirit-Father, or is he our Spirit-Father? Oh, what have we done that he is to take all from us that he had given us? His white children have come and have taken all our mountains, and all our valleys, and all our rivers; and now, because he has given us this little place without our asking him for it, he sends you here to tell us to go away."

Egan continued. "Do you see that high mountain away off there? There is nothing but rocks there. Is that where the Big Father wants me to go? If you scattered your seed and it should fall there, it will not grow . . . Oh, what am I saying? I know you will come and say: Here, Indians, go away; I want these rocks to make me a beautiful home with! . . . Tomorrow I am going to tell the soldiers what you are doing, and see if it is right."

Sarah, interpreting as fast as she could, clenched her hands tightly together. Egan is telling the truth, she thought. It is all true.

When at last Egan finished and sat down, Rinehart waited a moment, then addressed the gathering. "You had better all go and live with the soldiers . . . If you don't like what the government wants you to do, well and good; if I had it my way I could help you, but I cannot. I have to do government's will."

For all these months Sarah had protected Rinehart and kept her people from rising against him, but now she decided to fight him in the open. The next day she and Egan and several others went to nearby Camp Harney to ask for help.

"Write to Washington a full report," the officer advised.

Patiently Sarah toiled over her letter, and when it was done, the head chiefs signed it with their marks. Rinehart fired her.

So the happy times and the bad times at Malheur were over. Even though some of her people still were there, Sarah went away, and six months later when she returned to visit her cousin Jarry, the agent sent word that he didn't want her anywhere on the reservation.

She was alone again.

TEN

Sarah & Her Wagon
1878

FOR THE NEXT several months Sarah worked as maid in a private home on the other side of the Strawberry Mountains, saving her money, and buying a team and small wagon. Although she was temporarily separated from Indian unrest, it was growing, as thousands of settlers poured in. In one day three hundred wagons were counted on the Humboldt River. Wheat, barley, corn and oats grew in fenced fields in place of the waving native grass.

Natchez, who was farming in Nevada, had a statement printed that spring in the *Daily Silver State*. "My people are dying of diseases that they do not understand and cannot prevent. They are passing away like the snow

Camp Harney, army headquarters on the Malheur Reservation. Sarah rode to this fort several times seeking help from her soldier friends. OREGON HISTORICAL SOCIETY

on the mountains. Thirty-four of them have died within the last two or three months." Indian after Indian, in recorded interviews, told a tale of hunger and death.

About this time a Paiute named Wodziwob preached a new belief that all dead Indians would be resurrected, to unite and drive out the whites, and in this time of despair Wodziwob's doctrine spread like fire. The Bannocks of Idaho, who spoke the same language as the Paiutes, planned a great war involving all the tribes

and wanted the People to help them, but Winnemucca had repeatedly refused. However, in the spring of 1878, when he was farther south, a group of hungry Bannocks came again to Malheur. Even though Sarah was banished from the reservation, her people remembered that she had received the magic gift of education. Three times they sent messengers to her.

"Our poor children are crying to us for food, and we are powerless to help our little ones," they said, begging her to go to Camp Harney to plead with the officers, or, if that failed, to go all the way to Washington, D.C.

With little money and nothing from officials but a

long string of broken promises, Sarah felt helpless. However, at the third Paiute visit she promised to go to Malheur and meet with the chiefs. Poor as she was, and convinced the attempt would be useless, she felt she must try.

Before she started, two men from Canyon City asked to ride along, offering to pay their way. One had a daughter, and therefore, in early June Sarah took the two men and twelve-year-old Rosey in her wagon, over the summit to the reservation. She left them at the agent's house, then went on to that of her cousin Jarry, where she went to bed hungry because none of her friends had anything to eat.

Awakening in the night to the sound of voices, she found that Chiefs Egan and Oytes, and several Bannocks had come.

"Is Sarah asleep?" they asked. "We had better talk to her now for fear Rinehart will find out she is here and send her away, as he did before."

At once Sarah got up, to begin a council.

Their talk was of Agent Rinehart—of rebellion—and of food, always food. Some had gone to the fisheries in despair, but were able to catch very little. Egan said his people had almost nothing to eat, that whenever they received a little money, Rinehart's men gambled with them and took it away, for the Paiutes, to whom gambling was only a game, were easy prey. Bannocks spoke angrily of Rinehart's refusal to feed them, of rumors that all their horses were to be taken, of settlers who had seized the beautiful Idaho meadows where camas grew in abundance. The Indians had always depended on camas roots for food, and now it was lost.

On and on they talked, all the rest of the night, the next day, and another night. Oytes was determined to fight, but Egan had a different plan—to give Sarah their cash. "Let her go and talk for us," he urged. "Let her go right on to Washington, and have a talk with our Great Father."

Washington! Again they had spoken the thrilling name. Did Sarah, an Indian, a woman, dare to go so far and carry their story to the capital? Even if she dared, how could she accomplish it? Doubtfully, she agreed to try, at which they collected all the money they had— twenty-nine dollars and twenty-five cents.

With this, plus twenty-five dollars from twelve-year-old Rosey and her father, who wished to go on with her, Sarah set out again, intending to drive to Elko, Nevada, sell her horse and wagon there, and press on as best she could. Just as she started, the Paiute work hands—then Oytes—then all the rest of the Indians—left the reservation.

SHE NEVER FORGOT the silence of that trip, broken only by the clop-clop of her horses and rattle of wheels. She saw vacant houses along the road, and didn't know what they meant until the third day, at the summit, when a man told her of a great Indian war. The Bannocks, he said, were killing everyone who came their way. She must hurry on to a place called Stone House.

Swiftly she clattered along, going downhill now—

Places Important to Sarah during the Indian Wars and Later

1. Head of the John Day River, where Sarah lived and worked just before the Bannock War.
2. Malheur Reservation. (The borders are approximate.)
3. Camp Harney. Army post on the reservation.
4. Agency. Headquarters for the reservation.
5. Steens Mountain. (This is a very long, abrupt ridge.) Sarah's father was held prisoner here by the Bannocks.
6. Juniper Lake, where the escaping Paiutes assembled.
7. Sheep Ranch, where Sarah met Captain Bernard, and to which she returned after rescuing her father.
8. Camp Boise, army headquarters in the Bannock War. Sarah went to it as messenger for the army.
9. Big Camas Prairie, Idaho. The Bannock camas grounds that had been overrun by settlers, precipitating the Bannock War.
10. Camp McDermitt. Sarah had been interpreter there, and her father went there after his rescue.
11. Scene of Sarah's first big battle.
12. Simcoe Agency. Headquarters for Yakima Reservation.
13. Yakima Indian Reservation, where Leggins's band was taken. Sarah was interpreter and teacher there.
14. Yakima. The town whose newspaper editor publicized the plight of the Paiutes.
15. The Dalles, where Sarah was stranded after Father Wilbur refused to release her people.
16. Fort Vancouver, headquarters of General O. O. Howard, where Sarah became a teacher.

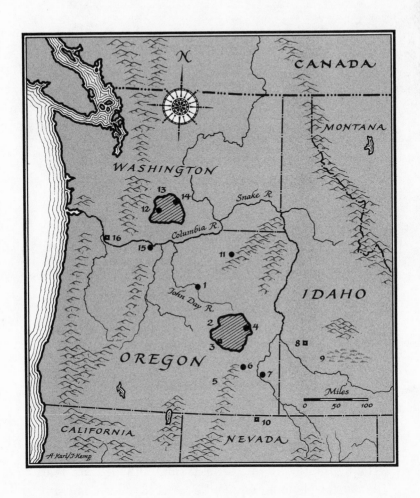

A unit of the United States Cavalry riding across the plains to engage in the Bannock War. AUTHOR

faster—faster. Nearly at the Oregon–Idaho border she was stopped by soldiers under command of Captain R. F. Bernard, who said the Bannocks were still fighting, and that she herself was in danger because she was thought to be carrying ammunition.

This terrified Sarah. "Go and see for yourself, Captain," she said, trying to keep calm although her heart seemed to bound into mouth. "And if you can find anything in my wagon besides a knife and fork, and a pair of scissors, I will give you my head for your football."

She told the captain everything—about the long

Paiute council, about her mission to Washington. She repeated, "Go to my wagon and see."

"No, Sarah, I believe you," the captain replied, letting her go free, while he mounted his horse and started for headquarters in Idaho.

That night Sarah wrestled with the problem of what to do, and by morning she had decided to abandon her trip. Twelve-year-old Rosey wept. Mr. Morton was dismayed. "Sarah, don't leave Rosey, for she has come to love you," he said, pleading with her to marry him. But she declined, told the soldiers she wanted to serve the army, and galloped to Fort Boise, where she found Captain Bernard again.

As she hoped, he had a job for her—a difficult one. Since some Paiute scouts were working for the army, the captain wanted her to ask them to take a message to Winnemucca, who was a prisoner in the Bannock camp.

Obediently she went to the scouts and delivered the message, but no matter how ardently she pleaded, they refused. "We will go anywhere but to the hostile Bannocks," they said, and told her Natchez had been killed trying to escape.

Hearing this, Sarah's heart felt dead within her. However, with Natchez gone, her people needed help more than ever before, and she must save them if she could. So she fought back her tears and reported to Captain Bernard. "The Indians won't go to the Bannocks, not for love or money. But Captain, I will go, if I have to go alone."

"Sarah! You cannot!" The captain was aghast.

"Yes, I will, if there is a horse to carry me." Sarah persisted until the captain reluctantly sent a telegram to General O. O. Howard, the commanding officer, to ask his consent.

General Howard, who remembered Sarah's help on his visit to Malheur, not only consented, he offered her a five-hundred-dollar reward. When they heard she was going, two of the Paiute scouts named John and George were ashamed of their own refusal and changed their minds. She would have an escort after all.

Crisply Captain Bernard explained that Winnemucca and his band, who had been at Fort McDermitt, had been asked to ride to Malheur Reservation and persuade the Paiutes there not to fight. On the way he had stopped at the Bannock camp, probably to urge them to make peace, but it was a mistake. The Bannocks, afraid Winnemucca and his men would fight against them, had carried off the whole group as prisoners. Sarah was now to find her father, assure him that the army wouldn't treat him as an enemy and would protect him from frightened settlers, who were ready to shoot any Indian on sight. She was to bring him back if she could.

"Go to your father," the captain said. "Tell him and his people that they shall be taken care of and be fed." He gave her a letter asking those she met along the way to help her.

Sarah knew this letter might prove a two-edged sword, ensuring aid from the settlers—or death from the Bannocks. But she thrust it into her pocket and mounted a swift army horse.

ELEVEN

Scout Sarah

1878

HOOFS THUDDED and hot wind blew their hair as Sarah, John and George galloped across the mountains, clambering up slopes and skidding down. The "hostiles" might lurk behind any rock.

Striking the Bannock trail, they pressed on until their horses stumbled in the dark. Then John and George took turns as sentinels, while Sarah tied her animal's rope to her arm, wrapped herself in a blanket, and lay down with her head on the saddle. She was awake most of the night, watching the black sky with its brilliant stars.

At dawn they were off again across the high semi-desert of eastern Oregon. Thirsty, hungry, they passed the still-smoking house of a burned-out ranch, and John shot a mountain sheep for food.

Steens Mountain. Sarah had to ride across this barren country
and climb these rugged slopes when she rescued her father.
OREGON STATE HIGHWAY COMMISSION

Late the second day, as the long blue blur of Steens
Mountain grew larger, they saw two riders and slowed
to a walk, ready to turn and run. However, in a moment
Sarah gasped with joy. One horseman was Lee, her

tall young brother, out hunting food, for there were
hundreds of hungry mouths in camp.

Thankfully the two embraced. "Where is our
father?" Sarah asked as soon as she could speak. "I must
go to him. I have a message."

"You will be killed!" Lee said, aghast. He explained
that Winnemucca was a prisoner, but that Natchez, who

had been captured and marked for death, had escaped just in time.

Alive! Sarah thought. Her dearest brother lived! When Lee implored her to turn back, she replied that she would go on, even if it meant death.

"Then take off your hat and dress, and unbraid your hair, and put your blanket around you," he said, helping her and her companions dress like Indians.

They began to climb the mountain, which was so steep they had to go on hands and knees. Rocks tore at their fingers, and brush pulled loose in their grasp. But at last they reached the ridge and peered over its edge, onto the encampment in a deep valley below.

"Oh, such a sight my eyes met!" Sarah later said. Spread over the valley were more than three hundred lodges, with warriors catching horses or killing beef, and blue smoke rising in the still air. It was so large—so strong! Dared she slip inside? Just as the sun was setting, she scrambled cautiously down and crept behind Lee to the Paiute section of the camp.

At Lee's low whistle she entered her father's tent and threw herself into his arms. He explained—hastily, in whispers—his attempt to pacify the Bannocks, their fear he would fight against them, and their capture of him and his band. He said Oytes had joined the Bannocks heart and soul, but most of the Paiutes had not.

"Come to the troops," Sarah pleaded, giving him the general's message.

Although Winnemucca was doubtful at first, he finally agreed to try, and together they devised a plan. Since the large camp required so much food, the Paiutes were allowed freedom to hunt and prepare it. Therefore, the women were to pretend to gather wood, slip away, catch horses, and wait at Juniper Lake on the other side of the mountain. As soon as it was dark, Sarah, with Winnemucca and the men, would follow.

Evening came. As they crept through the silent camp, Sarah was so fearful that she dropped flat to the ground at the sound of hoofbeats. But she heard a slow, soft, musical voice, and found it was Mattie, Lee's wife, bringing her a horse. Swiftly she mounted, and they all scrambled over the mountain to Juniper Lake, where Lee was waiting with the women. Winnemucca's party was now gathered ready to flee, while another group under Chief Egan was to follow, and Lee went back to rescue the rest.

All night they rode through the starlight, with six men in the rear as lookouts. At daybreak they stopped to rest—a short rest, for they heard an alarm and saw a man dashing toward them.

"We are followed by the Bannocks!" he shouted. "Egan and his whole band is overtaken!" He had seen Lee running, the Bannocks firing; and Lee had fallen to the ground.

At this, Chief Winnemucca was ready to give up, but Sarah was still resolute and knew she could make better time if she went on alone. So she decided to gallop ahead and ask General Howard for help. Just as she was about to leave, Mattie, weeping, cried out, "Let me go with you! If my poor husband is killed, why need I stay?"

"Come on!" Sarah replied, and leaning low on their

horses' necks, the two young women dashed away.

They had seventy-five miles to ride, with little water or food. They sang—prayed to the Great Father in the Spirit-land. Crossing a creek, they had a muddy drink and found some white currants to eat. At the home of a friendly settler they were given hard bread and coffee, and secured fresh horses.

Hair streaming, they pounded on, seeing columns of cavalry, artillery and infantry, half hidden by dust. It was just two years since Custer's troops had been annihilated in the famous "last stand," and one year since Chief Joseph's gallant retreat. Now the army was wheeling in from Arizona, California, Nevada, Utah, from Fort Vancouver in Washington, and from San Francisco. They meant to crush the Indians again.

Late in the afternoon Sarah and Mattie reached Sheep Ranch Camp, where Captain Bernard helped them off their horses, and Sarah burst into weeping. She had ridden almost constantly for three days, had traveled more than two hundred miles, and thought her brother was slain. But when General Howard came, she fought back her tears and told him where her father was, where the Bannocks were camped, and how many they numbered. To her joy, the general sent out troops, who found Winnemucca and took him safely to Fort McDermitt with nearly a hundred followers.

For the next three months, with Mattie at her side, Sarah was General Howard's interpreter, guiding him over "dim and dusty trails" for which he had no correct maps. He trusted her so completely that she belonged to the small group of about a dozen who traveled nearest to him.

At her first battle, in July, she thought every drop of blood in her veins would run out, and fully expected to die. The lines were so close that over the rumble of guns she could hear the Bannock chiefs singing, and once she heard Oytes shout, "Come on, you white dogs—what are you waiting for?"

Scouts of the United States Army and friendly Paiutes fighting on the same side in the Bannock War. AUTHOR

However, after the first bad moments she plunged forward. "Get behind the rocks, Sarah, you will be hit!" shouted General Howard.

She obeyed, but stayed at the front, and learned that her old friend, Chief Egan, who had tried and failed to escape with Winnemucca, had become the Bannocks' head chief. Hard as it must have been for Sarah to fight Egan, her friend and Mattie's uncle, she was still convinced that the Paiutes must cooperate with the white man—or die.

All through the mountain campaign Sarah rode near General Howard, crossing knife-edged divides and deep canyons, under a blazing sun or drizzly gray rain. When the horse-drawn commissary wagons were late, she was hungry. She interpreted signal fires, marked springs. Through her keen sight and hearing she pinpointed enemy locations. Once the general's scouts thought they saw an army of Indians on a facing hill, but Sarah recognized them as a trick of piling rocks to look like men. She helped care for the wounded. When a sergeant found an abandoned baby girl and fed it cookies, Sarah had it tended by Indian women, and later on located its Bannock parents, who gratefully named it Sarah.

In July, near the Blue Mountains of northern Oregon, Sarah slipped cautiously into the "hostile" camp at night, to try—in vain—to persuade the Paiutes to surrender. Shortly after that she had a nightmare in which she saw Egan murdered and his head cut off. The dream was so real that she screamed in her sleep until

Mattie wakened her. "Many of my family," she said, "have seen things in their dreams that were really happening."

This one came true. Within a short time a treacherous Umatilla named U-ma-pine quarreled with Egan over some horses and killed him, after which the Umatillas severed Egan's head and brought it to the army camp in a gunny sack. They sold it to an officer, after which, Sarah said, the camp doctor boiled it so he could keep the skull. The army itself later acknowledged that it was put on display.

With Egan slain, the Bannocks surrendered, and Sarah eagerly set out to visit her father at Camp McDermitt. When her soldier-escort was too slow to suit her, she galloped ahead and burst in, Sarah-fashion, with a whoop.

"Halloo! Get up! The enemy is at hand!" she shouted, laughing boisterously at her own joke, and leaping off her horse to embrace the startled Natchez. At finding Lee alive after all, her joy was complete.

When she told her father all she had done, he called his people together to inform them that she had fought in battle, while they had not. "Now hereafter we will look on her as our chieftain, for none of us are worthy of being chief but her," he said.

The Paiutes had never chosen a woman as chief, so this was an unprecedented honor for Sarah, an honor she had well earned. She was the one to whom the other Numa turned for help, the one the white men consulted. Even so, the title didn't stick. Those who knew her con-

Chief Winnemucca wearing a cast-off army uniform. This
was taken in Virginia City, after the Bannock War. NEVADA
HISTORICAL SOCIETY

tinued to call her just "Sarah," while the newspapers preferred "Princess."

Her next job was to travel from village to village, bringing the scattered Paiute bands to safety at Fort McDermitt, because settlers were ready to shoot any Indian on sight. She went to Idaho with the army, back to Oregon, covering hundreds of miles.

In October, officials in Washington ordered all Indians who had lived at Malheur to go to Camp Harney and from there to a reservation. Although Sarah trusted the army, some of the Paiutes didn't, and she met them at Camp McDermitt in a council that lasted all night. Should they obey—and risk starvation under Rinehart? Or should they refuse—and risk the soldiers' anger? Try as she might, Sarah couldn't persuade her father and Natchez to go, but one band under a young Chief Leggins agreed to obey, and Sarah went with them.

Although at first Leggins and his followers were not treated as prisoners, before long the commanding officer sent for Sarah, and there was something—in the messenger's eyes? in his voice?—something that made her heart jump. She hadn't felt like this since the night Egan was killed. Believing so strongly in premonitions, she trembled as she dressed and went down to the office.

"I felt sure something fearful was waiting," she said.

Leggins, whose band had never fought the whites, who himself had saved several settlers' lives, had come to Camp Harney at her urging, because he trusted her. He was in the army's power.

TWELVE

The Horror at Yakima
1878–1879

"SARAH," said the commanding officer when she walked into his office. "I have some news to tell you and I want you to keep it still until we are sure it is true."

"I will, if it isn't too awful bad news."

"It's pretty bad," he said, watching her closely. "Sarah, you look as if you were ready to die. It is nothing about you; it is about your people. Sarah, an order is issued that they are to be taken to Yakima Reservation, across the Columbia River."

"All of them?"

"No, not your father's people, but all that are here." He said he didn't know the reason.

Sarah's heart felt ready to burst, for Yakima lay far

to the north, in the opposite direction from Pyramid Lake. "Major, my people have not done anything," she said. "Why should they be sent away from their own country?" She remembered how she had coaxed them to come to Camp Harney. "Oh, Major! If you knew what I have promised my people, you would try not to have them sent away. Oh, Major! My people will never believe me again." She began to cry, even though the major said he would do his best to have the order revoked.

That evening, when she and Mattie strolled through the camp and heard Indians singing, she thought, "My poor, poor people, you will be happy today; tomorrow or next week your happiness will be turned to weeping." All night she lay awake, staring into the dark. But she didn't tell anyone except Mattie, because the major had asked her not to.

Days dragged by, frosty at first, then with heavy gray skies and snow. When at last the major again sent for Sarah, she was so frightened she could hardly stand. "Mattie, I wish this was my last day in this cruel world," she said. "I don't think I can walk down there alone."

"I will go with you."

Fearfully they entered the major's office, where he reluctantly told them the order had been confirmed, and that the people had just one week to get ready.

"What!" Sarah cried. "In this cold winter and in all this snow, and my people have so many little children? Why, they will all die. Oh, what can the President be thinking about? Oh, tell me, what is he? Is he man or beast?" She was nearly in tears. "I have never seen a president in my life, and I want to know whether he is made of wood or rock, for I cannot for once think that he can be a human being. No human being would do such a thing as that—send people across a fearful mountain in midwinter."

But much as he disliked the order, the major had no power to change it, and Sarah, who had again been warned not to tell her people, felt haunted. Every night she imagined she could see the thing called President, with long ears, big eyes, long legs, and a head like a bullfrog.

Three days before departure, when the Paiutes were informed of the trip, they were swept by panic. Some made a frantic dash for freedom. Others blamed Sarah for bringing them there. Even Lee and Leggins—her brother and her friend—refused to speak to her. Although she knew the fault was with officials in Washington, not with the army, Sarah felt betrayed. And still she was so convinced that rebellion would only bring worse punishment that she helped prepare for the journey. She rounded up all the fur-lined mittens and jackets she could, although the army didn't have enough to go around; and when Indians tried to escape, she helped bring them back.

One night when Sarah and Mattie went out with an officer to find five runaway women, Mattie's horse shied, throwing her off. To Sarah's horror, "the blood ran out of her mouth," and it seemed as if she might die at once. However, she was laid in an ambulance wagon, where she clung feebly to life.

At best the Yakima trip would mean great suffering, but an incredible official blunder made it infinitely worse. Rinehart, at Malheur, expecting the Paiutes to be sent there, had ordered and received ample winter supplies, including warm clothes and sixty thousand pounds each of beef and flour. Although these were only fifty-five miles away, although the army reported that the women and children were "destitute and suffering for want of clothing," the People weren't allowed to wait until the sorely needed goods could come. Comfortable officials in warm houses three thousand miles away had decided that all "hostiles" must be removed so far from their homes that they couldn't ever return to start more trouble, and that they must set out at once.

Nor would the officials bother to separate friends from enemies. Both settlers and officers testified that young Chief Leggins had kept the peace and saved white men's lives, and still a telegram from Washington specifically said he and his band must go too. This meant that Mattie, injured as she was, had to make the trip. Again settlers and officers protested, but in vain. Stern orders came, which the army had to obey, and just after Christmas the tragic caravan set out in fifty wagons. Men, women and children sat on hay and furs covered with tarpaulins, while settlers drove and two companies of cavalry were escorts. They were to travel three hundred fifty miles, over two mountain ranges, and cross a turbulent river in open boats.

Every night for more than a month they camped in the snow with only canvas tents for shelter. Two babies were born and died, along with one of the mothers, and three other children and an old man were frozen to death. Unable to transport the dead or dig graves in the frozen ground, the soldiers had to toss the bodies aside for wolves to devour.

When they reached Yakima, nothing was ready to receive them, because the agent, generally called Father Wilbur, had not known they were coming until sixteen hours before their arrival. He said it was "a Marvel of Marvels" that he hadn't been notified sooner, and asked, "How are they to be subsisted? Where is the money to meet the expense? . . . We have Beef Cattle, but they belong properly to the Indians of the Agency, and Cannot in justice be used for hostile bands that may be moved here."

After meeting them in their desolate camp, and seeing their hollow cheeks, their rags and tatters, he sent the commissioner a frantic wire. "Five hundred & forty three Snake & Piute indians arrived yesterday without official notice of their coming. in a destitute condition Nearly Naked something must be done immediately to feed and clothe them answer by telegram."

It was small comfort to realize that the warehouses at Malheur were crammed—with not a single Indian there.

Hastily Father Wilbur had a building put up to house them, one hundred fifty feet long by seventeen feet wide, slightly less than five square feet per person. Although he said it would "give them comfortable quarters for the winter." Sarah called it a shed such as

Father Wilbur, agent at Yakima Reservation. At first he was Sarah's friend, but later turned against her. AUTHOR

would be used for cattle, and it must have been just that, for it had been built in a single day.

"Oh, how we did suffer with cold," Sarah wrote. "There was no wood, and the snow was waist-deep, and many died off just as cattle or horses do after travelling so long in the cold."

This was a large reservation established for the Yakima Indians, who had been Wilbur's wards for many years. They had snug houses and a rudimentary education, while the Paiutes, in rags and unable to speak the language, were living in the shed. Traditional enemies of the People, the Yakimas resented the appropriation of their supplies. They gambled with the Paiutes for their warm army jackets and seized every chance to steal what few horses the Paiutes had managed to bring along. Although Sarah complained and agents' reports acknowledged this, nothing was done to stop it.

In the spring Father Wilbur sent out seventeen wagons, which soon came lurching in, loaded with the Malheur blankets, shawls, woven goods and calicoes. But there still weren't enough. Sarah wrote in her autobiography:

"Issuing day came. It was in May. Poor Mattie was so sick, I had to go by myself to issue to my people. Oh, such a heartsickening issue! There were twenty-eight little shawls given out, and dress-goods that you white people would sift flour through, from two to three yards to each woman. The largest issue was to a woman who had six children. It was six yards, and I was told to say to her she must make clothes for the children out of what was left after she had made her own!"

On May 29, after months of suffering, gentle, soft-voiced little Mattie died, leaving Sarah bitterly certain that, if her young friend had received better care, she would have lived. But she toiled on, and when they saw how hard she was working, her people forgave her for leading them there. She interpreted for them and taught a school for Paiute children, all without salary.

"Out of what fund is she to be paid?" Father Wilbur asked the Bureau. "She has done a noble work in the school room, out of the school, instructing the Paiute women and girls how to cut and make garments for the children of the Paiute School, and themselves, and doing me essential service as interpreter." He also said her pupils—"35 Schollers"—were making astonishing progress in their studies but "they are nearly naked and greatly in need of books, charts, etc. Probably from 80 to 100 would gladly attend school if I had the means to supply even the scantiest clothing."

In the fall he wrote again, "I want to know where the Beef and Flour is Coming from, or rather where the Money is to Meet Said Expenses!! I Confess it looks foggy to me . . . the winter is fast approaching and what is done must be done *immediately* or our roads will be blocked with snow."

By the spring of 1879, when the Paiutes had been there more than a year, Wilbur had received only four thousand dollars for their support, which he estimated had cost three times that amount. Sarah's position as interpreter and teacher had not been confirmed, nor her salary paid, nor had she received her promised reward for rescuing her father.

She had a revenge of sorts when a camp meeting was held with visitors from the East.

"Be sure to keep your people away," Father Wilbur told her, "because they are very poorly dressed."

This was sadly true. Seizing the chance, Sarah brought her nearly naked followers to meeting, and had them sit on the benches for everyone to see.

She struck a stronger blow in November, when at last the five hundred dollars reward arrived. Since her people had been begging her almost daily to go east and speak for them, and since she now had the means, she secured Father Wilbur's permission, and left.

Her first stop was Fort Vancouver, to see her old friend General O. O. Howard, who gave her a letter of introduction to other army officers.

Next she went to San Francisco, where she embarked on a brand new career. Knowing that audiences were interested in Indians, she hired a hall for a series of lectures. It was a daring move for a woman without backers—and it worked. Sarah was a sensation.

Thirty-five years old, but looking much younger, "well-formed and graceful," she put on a good show. She had the stage decorated to represent a forest, with three Paiute braves seated in the background, and she herself splendid in a long feathered head dress, cape and short skirt of buckskin, blue beads, embroidered moccasins, and bright red stockings. In dramatic detail she described the life of her people before the whites came, their recent sufferings, the causes of the War of 1860, and the cruelties of agents, Rinehart in particular. She

Sarah as she appeared when she spoke in San Francisco.

was so sincere and spoke with so much feeling—eyes flashing, sometimes weeping—that many of her audience wept with her. Although her vocabulary was plain and her sentences generally short, one reporter said the "simple beauty" of her speech was similar to that of "Holy Writ." (The Bible.)

She was frequently interrupted. "If your people will help us . . . I will promise to educate my people and make them law-abiding citizens of the United States." (Loud applause.) "It can be done—it can be done." (Cheers.)

Sometimes she concluded by singing an Indian song, or with a dance by her painted braves.

By her farewell address on December 23, she realized how effective she could be, and said she was going East to lecture. "I will expose all the rascals. I will save nobody. I will name the paths, the officer, the Agent . . . My mouth shall not be sealed."

It happened that Special Agent J. M. Haworth of the Office of Indian Affairs was in Nevada just then, to try to find out why the Indians refused to go to Malheur. He had already met several chiefs, who told him repeatedly, in the strongest words, that they trusted no agents, and especially not Rinehart.

"Leggins' party saved you but you sent him to Yakima," protested Sarah's father. "You make paper lie when you read it."

Natchez backed him. "I heard you read paper two ways, and we can not trust you."

Winnemucca continued, "You promise us good

things, but your promises are very forked. They branch out in many different directions."

And another said, "You have contracts from which you want to make money starving the Indians."

Hearing of Sarah's plan to lecture in the East, Haworth was determined to block it, so he invited her, Winnemucca, Natchez and a cousin to make the trip as guests of the government.

With high hopes she prepared for the journey to Washington, the promised land, the city of the Big Father who could make everything right at last.

But the Bureau of Indian Affairs had its own reasons for paying her way.

THIRTEEN

Forked Promises
1880–1883

A S SARAH RODE to Washington, that winter of 1880, she had every right to feel pleased and proud, and excited too, for she was going to meet the Great Father, President Hayes himself. She wanted two things: the release of Leggins's band from Yakima; food and land for the Paiutes.

She, Winnemucca, Natchez and a cousin named Captain Jim jolted along, sitting up day and night for a week, and catching what little sleep they could. They crossed the Rocky Mountains, the Mississippi River, the forested Appalachians, and on January 19, they entered the nation's capital.

While Winnemucca was head chief in name, Sarah was the real leader of the group, partly because of her excellent English, partly because of her natural fire. She

The Winnemucca family, taken while they were in
Washington, D.C. From left to right they are: Sarah, Chief
Winnemucca, Natchez (standing), another member of the
tribe, and a white boy who sometimes served as their guide.
NATIONAL ARCHIVES

Carl Schurz, Secretary of the Interior when Sarah visited
Washington, D.C. She felt that he double-crossed her.
NATIONAL ARCHIVES

was the one who talked most with officials, the one
sought by reporters. However, the Bureau of Indian
Affairs tried to muzzle her by keeping her busy sightsee-
ing from morning to night and giving her little chance
to meet reporters. One newsman who managed an inter-
view was favorably impressed by her "neat-fitting black
suit with satin facings and trimmings," and said she be-
haved "as much like a lady as anyone there." A lady
Sarah might be, but she boldly described her people's
plight and threatened that if they didn't get relief, they
would bring charges against the Bureau—"Charges that
we will prove."

Although she met President Hayes, she had no
chance to talk with him, for he was in and out of the
room before she could catch her breath. Her main con-
tact was Carl Schurz, Secretary of the Interior, which
was the department in charge of Indian affairs.

"So you are bound to lecture," Schurz said to her, at
one of their interviews.

"People want me to."

He said she had no right to do so, since she had
come at government expense, but offered to grant all she
asked, including canvas for tents. "You can issue it, can
you not?"

"Yes, if it comes."

"We will send enough to make your people one
hundred tents," he promised, and arranged to ship them
to Lovelock, Nevada, as soon as she returned home.
More than that, at their last meeting he handed her an
order which provided all she desired: one hundred sixty

acres of land for the head of each Paiute family, and freedom for Leggins's band. Sarah was so buoyed up by success that she insisted on a sleeping car for the return trip.

In Lovelock the Indians, who heard about the tents and gathered to receive them, waited day after day for canvas that didn't come. They were hungry. When Sarah wrote to Secretary Schurz, "for God's sake send us

Snow plow of the Central Pacific Railroad (now the Southern Pacific) in the high mountains. When Sarah went to Washington, D.C., she passed through drifts like these.
AUTHOR

something to eat," he told her to take her people to
Malheur—but didn't suggest how they could travel more
than three hundred miles without money or food,
through drifted snow.

Some of the Paiutes jeered. Others accused her of
making up the promise of tents, and even when Sarah
read them the order, they thought she was lying.

One of her uncles stepped forward. "I have lived
many years with white people, and I have never known
one of them do what they promised," he said. "I think
they mean it just at the time, but I tell you they are very
forgetful. It seems to me, sometimes, that their memory
is not good . . . They are a weak people."

The Indians then drifted back to their wretched
homes, to live out the winter as best they could. Winnemucca had once told Haworth, "Your promises are
very forked," and now Sarah again realized this bitter
truth.

But she still had the order for Leggins's release, so
on April first—April Fools' Day—she started for
Yakima, several hundred miles away, accompanied by
Natchez's wife. Hard as the trip would be, Sarah was
buoyed up by thought of Leggins's joy at being set free.
She and her sister-in-law set out, traveling north. They
were helped along the way by many kindhearted people,
Indian and white, who supplied food and horses.

At Camp Harney, on the old Malheur Reservation,
the snow was so deep they waited for ten long days before tackling the Blue Mountains. "Oh, such a time as
we had going over!" Sarah said. "The snow was soft

—our horses would go down and up again. If we walked, we would go down too." Sometimes it rained, churning the snow to slush and soaking their long skirts. At one stream they had to swim their horses, and by the time they reached Canyon City they were almost frozen.

Here Sarah had a few hours of pure pleasure, for she saw Mr. Parrish, her beloved agent, and showed him the papers from Secretary Schurz. Parrish was almost as elated as she.

Although Sarah was out of money, she was able to borrow some on strength of her appointment as interpreter, and for the last leg of their journey they rode the "stage"—a rough wagon, barely big enough to hold them. Mile after mile for two weary days they bumped along, and at The Dalles they hired horses for another two days' ride. When at last, on May 8, they rode into Fort Simcoe, on Yakima Reservation, they had been on the road for more than five weeks.

Sarah's first step was to report to Father Wilbur, who seemed glad to see her, but soon dashed all her hopes, for he had received no orders from Washington.

"That is strange—they told me they would write right off," she said, bewildered, as she handed him the papers. "Father, I have a letter here, which Secretary Schurz gave me."

It worked no magic. Father Wilbur read it, turned stiff with anger, and said the Paiutes were perfectly contented at Yakima, and she mustn't stir them up by telling them of the letter. Even so, her people heard of it and called her in.

Leggins had been young and strong when she knew him, but now he was bent and going blind. "We are all told that she has a paper, which has been given to her by the mighty Big Father in Washington, and she has burnt it, or hid it, so we won't know it," he said. "She first sold us to the soldiers and had us brought here, and now she has sold us to this bad man to starve us." Tears ran down his face. "There is nobody to talk for us, we are all alone."

Lee knew about Sarah's meeting with the agent. "For shame! What are you talking about?" he shouted to Leggins. "Are you mad? Go and talk to Father Wilbur, not to my sister. It is he who has sold us!" Many were weeping.

Sarah, betrayed by the whites and despised by her own, held up the paper. What though Father Wilbur had asked her to keep it secret? Officials had played her false, over and again. "You have a right to say I have sold you. It looks so," she said. "I have told you more lies than I have hair on my head . . . They were the words of the white people, not mine." Her voice rose. "I have suffered everything but death to come here with this paper. I don't know whether it speaks truth or not." Word by word she read aloud all its promises, at which her people forgave her. Jumping about and laughing with glee, they made plans to leave immediately, and called on Father Wilbur for help.

He refused. Sending for Sarah, he told her the Paiutes had been contented until she came to stir them up. Disappointed as she was, Sarah managed to keep her temper until he accused her of putting the devil into her people's heads. Then she threw aside caution.

"Mr. Wilbur, you forget that you are a Christian when you can talk so to me," she lashed out. "You are starving my people here, and you are selling the clothes which were sent to them. That is why you want to keep us here, not because you love us. I say, Mr. Wilbur, everybody in Yakima City knows what you are doing, and hell is full of just such Christians as you are."

"Stop talking or I will have you locked up."

"I don't care . . . My people are saying I have sold them to you and get money from you to keep them here. I am abused by you and by my own people, too." Sarah stood her ground. "Mr. Wilbur, you will not get off as easily as you think you will. I will go to Yakima City and lecture."

From this day on, Father Wilbur was Sarah's unrelenting enemy. Earlier, his reports had praised her "noble work," and pleaded for funds to pay her. Now they called Schurz's letter "a somewhat indefinite written promise," (although it was actually specific), accused Sarah of securing it "doubtless through misrepresentation," spoke of her "disreputable intrigues," and said, "she is utterly unreliable and no dependence whatever can be placed on her character or her word."

Abandoning attempts to get along with the Bureau, Sarah vowed to get her people off the reservation by whatever means she could. But in order to do that, she must figure out a way for them to pass through the settlements without being shot. So she told her story to the editor of the Yakima City paper, who printed her accusations and those of the Paiute head men.

Fifty-eight had died the first winter at Yakima, including thirty children, they said, and while at first they could bury them, they later had to throw the bodies into the water courses. The editor, who had investigated, said he had "not a particle of doubt of Sarah's story, nor had anyone who knew Indian affairs at Yakima." Reminding his readers that Sarah had always been a firm friend to the whites, he told them that she and Lee were planning to lead their people in an escape, stopping occasionally to hunt game. "She pledges her own life for the peaceable intentions and good conduct of her people and hopes her white brothers and sisters will not molest them."

Forceful as the editorial was, it was only one of many that were printed year after year in newspapers of the West, telling their readers of the mistreatment of Indians.

Not one to give up easily, Father Wilbur next offered Sarah a free ride to The Dalles where, he suggested, she could wait for the rest of the Paiutes. It was a trick. As soon as she left, he sent a telegram to the Commissioner of Indian Affairs, asking whether to hold her people or let them leave, and recommending that they be held. As he expected, the reply said he should keep them there, and with Sarah out of the way he managed to do it.

So she was stranded in The Dalles. Her people didn't come. She was far from her father in Nevada and had no money. In despair she wrote to General O. O. Howard, her old friend of Bannock War days, who gave her a position as teacher and interpreter at Fort Vancouver, where several groups of Idaho Indians were being held prisoner. This, she thought, would probably be her last government post, for from now on she meant to work openly against the Bureau.

While she was at Fort Vancouver, General Howard sent an investigator, A. Chapman, to Yakima Reservation, and Chapman reported that the Paiutes were truly starving, that "a more destitute people I never met," and that he went into their tents to see if they had anything hidden away but found nothing. Chapman's report was sent to Washington, with a reminder from army officers that Leggins's band had never been hostile, and Father Wilbur's own statements confirmed that he had them on "short rations." But the Bureau sent no help.

In 1882, after Sarah had spent two years at Fort Vancouver, she went to visit her sister Elma, who was still married and living in Montana. While she was there, Sarah herself was married again, to Lambert Hopkins, a good-looking white man, several years younger than she, but without much firmness of character. However, they spent a tranquil year in Montana, removed from the problems of Leggins and his band.

That summer two hundred Paiutes crossed the Columbia in an attempt to escape—a vain attempt, for Father Wilbur had them overtaken and brought back. Although he said he did it because it would be dangerous for them to go unescorted through the settlements,

Lambert Hopkins, Sarah's husband. NEVADA HISTORICAL SOCIETY

Sarah was sure he wanted to hold them so he could draw more of their goods.

She received other sad news in the fall, for her father fell seriously ill and died. While the Paiutes were an honest people, intelligent and generally kind, they fiercely upheld a severe moral code. The tribe, and Winnemucca too, believed · his young wife had bewitched him, causing his death. Therefore they took her to a lonely spot on the desert, tied her to a stump, and stoned her to death.

Even though she was living in distant Montana, Sarah couldn't escape her people's troubles for long. She visited them again at Pyramid Lake, and when they urged her to go east once more and talk for them, she consented.

This time she wouldn't try to work through Bureau officials, or the president, or her army friends.

She was going to appeal to the nation.

FOURTEEN

A Different Kind of Battle
1883–1884

BOSTON was a center of culture, where it was a triumph to be accepted, and early in 1883 Sarah —daughter of the desert, with only three weeks of formal schooling—went there and promptly became its darling. Dr. Buchanan of Boston University introduced her at one lecture; for two weeks she was houseguest in the home of Mrs. Ole Bull, widow of a famous violinist; Senator Henry L. Dawes wrote a letter of support to be read at one of her meetings. Her most enthusiastic admirers were two intellectual, elderly sisters, Elizabeth Palmer Peabody and Mary Peabody Mann, who made Sarah's cause their own. Well known and highly re-

Mary Peabody Mann, who edited Sarah's book *Life Among the Paiutes, Their Wrongs and Claims*. MASSACHUSETTS HISTORICAL SOCIETY

Elizabeth Palmer Peabody of Boston, who was Sarah's staunch friend. LIBRARY OF CONGRESS

spected, they helped her set up lectures, introduced her to their friends, and arranged publicity—lots of it.

Sarah dressed for the platform in a costume that outshone even the fanciful trappings of her San Francisco lectures. Now thirty-nine years old but smooth-faced and attractive, she "was richly and fantastically attired" in buckskin trimmed with sparkling beads and shells, while armlets and bracelets gleamed on her arms and wrists. At her side hung a little velvet bag embroidered with a Cupid, and on her head was a crimson crown, ornate with stars and brilliants. Easterners gaped —and listened.

Speaking without notes and relying on the inspiration of the moment, Sarah gave lectures in several cities. Elizabeth Peabody said she heard her more than thirty times, and that each lecture contained something new. Sarah didn't charge admission, but asked for volunteer contributions, generally holding a first meeting for women only, which practically assured a crowd. Westerners had often spoken of the Paiutes' high moral standards. Now Sarah explained that these were due to the careful upbringing of girls, who were forbidden even to talk to any man except their fathers and brothers. Some listeners may have been disappointed, for one of them wrote, "There was nothing in it to . . . contaminate the most innocent young man."

In San Francisco Sarah had given only single lectures, but now she planned a connected series. When she couldn't sell enough tickets for that, she blithely decided to write a book that would give a complete background for her lectures to fill in. It would also earn expenses and enable her to bank the free-will offerings. What if she had little schooling, wrote slowly and painfully, and had to maintain a demanding schedule of lectures? She would find the time for it, somehow.

In spite of her skimpy education, Sarah had several qualities important to an author—eloquence, devotion to her subject, a phenomenal memory, and above all, a will of iron. She had lived with the Ormsby family, had bought and studied grammar books, had worked for years as interpreter, thus gaining much practice with the English language. She had already written excellent letters and articles, and now she retold many stories that she had used in her lectures, such as a description of the journey to Yakima. Although this helped greatly, writing a book was hard. She bent to her manuscript, sticking to it until the job was done, and laboring so earnestly that her friend and editor, Mary Peabody Mann, called it "an heroic act," and said she corrected only the spelling and punctuation.

Writing from memory, Sarah made mistakes in details, especially in dates, and she sometimes blamed individual agents for the faults of the Bureau. But she told the story of her people honestly and vividly, as she remembered it. Hers was the first book published by an Indian in the English language.

While she toiled over it, Sarah continued to speak in city after city, including sixty-six times in Baltimore alone. With her trembling voice, flashing eyes, and tears, she was as effective with eastern audiences as she had been in San Francisco. They wept with her, and often listeners, including a professor, a minister, and two priests, stood up spontaneously to say they had lived in the West and knew she was telling the truth.

Wherever she went she circulated a petition to the United States Congress, pleading for her people to be given Malheur Reservation, to receive land as individuals, and for Leggins's band to be set free. The petition reminded Congress that the Secretary of the Interior had already promised all this, but the promise had not been fulfilled. Persuasive Sarah got thousands of signatures and appeared before a Congressional Committee.

When they realized how effective Sarah was, the Bureau of Indian Affairs began to fight back. Three years earlier, when she went to Washington, Rinehart thought she was going to have him fired, and he had then forwarded several affidavits that claimed she was a drunkard, immoral, and untruthful. Now, instead of trying to disprove Sarah's charges, the Bureau dug out these old affidavits, and printed them in its magazine *Council Fire*. Calling her a "tool" in the army's struggle to regain control of Indian affairs, it made wild accusations, none of which it backed up by reputable sources.

"She is so notorious for her untruthfulness as to be wholly unreliable," trumpeted the *Council Fire*. "She is known to have been for some time an inmate of a house of ill-fame in the town of Winnemucca, Nevada, and to have been a common camp follower consorting with common soldiers."

This started a storm. Calling the attack "an un-

Sarah in the costume she wore while lecturing in Boston.

pardonable crime," Mrs. Mann said, "a purer, nobler soul than her own I have never met." A judge from Winnemucca wasn't quite so flowery, but said he had known Sarah since 1869 and had never heard her truthfulness or morals questioned.

Her most emphatic defender was the editor of the Winnemucca *Silver State*, who knew her well. He wrote, "Because she states before an audience in Boston what the whites in Nevada and on the frontier generally know to be facts, the *Council Fire* roundly abuses her." He bluntly accused the Bureau of cheating, starving and mistreating the Indians, and said its inhuman policies frequently drove them to the warpath.

"No agent has had the hardihood to publicly deny her statement through the newspapers or before an audience west of the Rocky Mountains," he said. "The *Council Fire* ought to know that scandalous charges against this woman, based on false affidavits of rascally Indian agents and their paid tools, are not arguments, and are no answer to her indictment of these agents."

Never would Sarah lie down under attack. Gathering two dozen letters from three generals and many other officers and prominent people, she used them as an appendix to her book, which was about to go to press. Some of the letters confirmed her service to the army and rescue of her father from the Bannocks, while others upheld her character.

This public scrap brought audiences, book buyers, and signers to her petition, and Sarah emerged triumphant. In the summer of 1884, when she had been in the

East just over a year, the Senate passed a bill that promised freedom to the Paiutes at Yakima and granted them land. However, it was too late to give them Malheur Reservation, for that had already been opened to white settlers.

It was also too late to help the Indians at Yakima, who had slipped away again to cross the Columbia River. By this time Father Wilbur had retired, and his successor didn't try to stop them. Although Wilbur had insisted that the Paiutes were contented there until Sarah stirred them up, the new agent bluntly said this wasn't so.

All this time Sarah had been lecturing and saving every penny, for she had another dream—of a school for Indian children, taught by Indians themselves, a school that would train its students as teachers for their own people. Up to then, Indian schools, both private and under the Bureau, had been taught and managed by white people who tried to "civilize" the students by wiping out native language and culture. Sarah, however, was sure her people's culture was worth preserving.

Now, with the Senate bill passed, the Commissioner of Indian Affairs, Hiram Price, urged her to go back to Nevada and sent her a letter promising cooperation. Another letter, from Adjutant General John C. Kelton, said the army had cleared the Pyramid Lake Reservation of white trespassers, and that Sarah must come and lead her people upon it.

Therefore, with money at hand and apparent help from the government, she decided to return home. In the summer of 1884, carrying her precious savings, she and her husband boarded the train for Wadsworth, Nevada, at the edge of the Reservation, where she would take up her new duties as teacher. Her husband was not well, but she was going to a free people, and a job, and security.

The first disaster overtook her before she got there. She was robbed of most of her money.

The second disaster fell when she met Natchez on the train, on his way to gather pine nuts, and learned he was being threatened with a jail sentence for a debt he hadn't incurred. Horrified, unwilling to let her brother go to prison, Sarah gave him what little she had left. After all, she thought, she would soon have her teacher's salary to live on.

As she and her ailing husband alighted from the train, her dream was still intact.

But a third disaster was waiting.

FIFTEEN

The Indian
Joan of Arc
1884–1891

CONFIDENTLY Sarah went to the agency to begin teaching—and the agent refused her the job. It had been a dizzying fall. Only a few weeks before, she had been sought after, admired, a successful author and lecturer, heard by Congress. Now she was stranded with no money and no work. Able to think of only one source of help—Natchez—she hurried to the town of Winnemucca, where she found his circumstances as beggarly as her own. As a last resort she wired Miss Peabody in Boston for whatever profits had accumulated from sales of her book, and received fifty dollars.

With this she settled down to face the winter. Her husband was ill with tuberculosis, the disease that had claimed so many of her tribe; Sarah herself developed pneumonia; most of Natchez's family fell sick and his oldest son died. Later Elizabeth Peabody called those months a "martyrdom from starvation, cold, and the resulting sickness." Sarah considered lecturing in California to earn money to buy a few acres where she might start her school, but she hadn't strength to make the effort. Her tribe was having trouble, too. As soon as the army left the reservation, white squatters returned, and Secretary Schurz, whom she had met in Washington, played her false again by ignoring the congressional bill that was supposed to give the Indians land.

However, Senator Leland Stanford, who later established Stanford University, had for many years been interested in Indian problems. Hearing about the plucky Indian princess and her brother the chief, he gave Natchez one hundred sixty acres of land near Lovelock, Nevada.

With this gift of land Sarah decided not to fight the Bureau longer, but start the school on her own. She lectured again in San Francisco, carrying a little black silk handkerchief to dry her tears, and presenting Natchez and half a dozen braves as dancers.

"What I say for my people is so written on my heart that it will never be washed out, never while I live upon this cruel world," she said, and pleaded for her people to receive the right to vote. Although ladies crowded around after the lectures to shake her hand, she didn't raise enough money for the school, so she appealed to friends in the East, who sent her seven hundred dollars.

Natchez, Sarah's brother. They were closely associated all
their lives, and Sarah established her school on Natchez's
farm. NEVADA HISTORICAL SOCIETY

With this Natchez fenced his ground and bought a wagon, plough, spade, hoe, axe, and other tools. While he cleared the land, Sarah started out bravely as teacher, plunging into her new role with the same zest she had shown as scout, lecturer, and writer. Nothing was too difficult, nothing was too much trouble. Sarah had always loved children and gotten along well with them, and by fall, 1885, young Indians could be seen in the morning carrying their lunches to her school, where she held classes in a brush arbor, The pupils—aged six to sixteen—were so eager to learn that they wrote their new English words all over the fences of Lovelock and taught them to their delighted parents.

By January, Natchez had a building under roof, partly as a house, partly for the school, on which Sarah proudly emblazoned its name—"Peabody Institute." Since her only furniture was benches without backs, her pupils used these as tables, and sat or knelt on the floor, or even lay on it to write and work arithmetic. Sarah read to them in English and Paiute from the best books she could find, including the Bible.

Shortly after she opened the new building, seven curious Lovelock citizens came to visit, and were "spellbound" at what they found. "When we neared the school shouts of merry laughter rang upon our ears, and little dark and sunburnt faces smiled a dim approval of our visitation," they wrote Miss Peabody. They were astonished to hear the students name objects in English, recite the days of the week and months of the year, calculate numbers "to thousands," and sing gospel hymns.

Successful as it was, the school would have to be scattered for the summer, when parents must take their children along on the yearly hunt for seeds and nuts. Since Sarah couldn't afford to feed them, Miss Peabody contributed money and advertised for more donations, which came flooding in. Assured of one hundred dollars a month for the summer, Sarah then changed over to a boarding school, with her pupils to help with house and farm work. She took nothing for herself except expenses.

As she continued to lecture in Nevada and California, Sarah's fame grew. Indians followed her through the streets and were delighted when she paused to clasp their outstretched hands. White people, both men and women, came to hear what she had to say.

Her talks were vivid, detailed, salty. Calling a certain agent a gambler, she said, "I will do him credit of saying he is a square gambler." Asked what she thought about having a gambler as agent, she replied, "I would rather have a gambler than a preacher with a bottle in one pocket and Bible in the other."

She was also gaining national notice. "Out in Nevada is proceding an experiment that deserves the respectful sympathy of the world," the *Daily Alta California* said, while editors of other newspapers wrote, "The Princess Sarah is making her school for young Paiutes a success." "We believe that the Indian Department should found an Indian school in Nevada and put Sarah at the head of it." Another thought the government should be told of the school, so she might "have facilities equal to her energy and to her noble spirit."

Naturally, the Bureau heard about Sarah's school, and—naturally—they were not pleased. One day an official appeared in Lovelock to say that unless Natchez surrendered his ownership of the land, and unless Sarah allowed the "authorized" agent of Pyramid Lake to direct her school, she would receive no aid from the reserved fund for Indian education. Having gotten along this far without government help, she indignantly refused.

In summer a Wisconsin schoolteacher who came to study Sarah's methods found the pupils in the second primer and superior to many white children in freeness of speech, in writing and drawing. She was impressed because the boys were learning practical skills by digging a cellar after study hours, while the girls assisted in cooking and cleaning. But Sarah herself was ill with rheumatism and neuralgia, chills and fever. Although her visitor stayed a month and dosed her with quinine, which cooled the fever, the pain lingered, making it a misery to get through each day.

In addition to her illness, Sarah was facing financial problems that threatened to swamp her. First, a misguided friend of Miss Peabody wrote that the kindly Easterner had spent money she needed for her old age, to help pay expenses. "She's been working for you to get the $100 a month, harder than you have ever worked in your life," the letter said.

Horrified, Sarah decided to keep a day school only; she could manage that without imposing on her friend.

Next, some neighboring farmers who resented

Indian ownership of land managed to have Natchez's irrigation water cut off. They also convinced his Indian helpers that the money from the East had been sent for them, not the school, and persuaded the workmen to demand their pay at once, in cash.

"If we could have borrowed $200 for two months, we could have paid them in money, and then sold the rest of the crop for $30 a ton," Sarah wrote to Miss Peabody. "But it was the game to force us to sell the crop to the storekeepers for $17 a ton, which (thanks to the Spirit Father for so much) paid all our debts, but left nothing over; and I could not feed on love."

Even Sarah, with all her vitality and determination, couldn't surmount so many obstacles. She said she was "perfectly discouraged and worn out," hoped that "the Spirit Father may soon let me die," and ended, "So, darling, do not talk any more on my behalf, but let my name die out and be forgotten; only, don't you forget me, but write to me sometimes, and I will write to you while I live."

She was forced to close the school.

Again her friends rallied. Assuring her that the money for her old age was untouched, Miss Peabody took charge of collecting funds, which enabled Sarah to reopen in the fall, and she continued for another year, honored by white and Indians alike. If she had had the means, she might have founded a large establishment, for the parents of four hundred Paiute children asked Natchez to take them to board, "where they could be really taught."

However, Sarah's husband died of tuberculosis; a beloved niece, Delia, also died of the same disease, and in 1887, heartbroken, Sarah abandoned her school again, this time for good.

For her last four years she lived in obscurity. Still a hearty Paiute, she loved to meet with her people, feast and drink with them. Sometimes she sat on the ground in a boisterous gambling game, throwing the cards or tossing the sticks and shouting with laughter. She was still the white man's friend. One newspaper story mentions her as part of a rowdy group, but says hers was the voice that stopped the rest from doing harm.

One of the People, named Wovoka, had revived the old belief in the resurrection of Indians, and red men of many nations—Paiute, Ute, Bannock, Shoshone, Cheyenne, Sioux—were wearing "ghost shirts" while they sang and danced in a fervor that would eventually lead to the Battle of Wounded Knee. But Sarah was too ill to be part of it.

For a while she worked as maid in a white household, earning money to go to her sister Elma in Montana. There, on October 17, 1891, Sarah Winnemucca—Princess Sarah, Chief Sarah—was taken with a sudden pain and died, probably of tuberculosis acquired from her husband. She was only forty-seven years old.

But her work didn't die with her, for thousands of influential people had heard her lectures, or read her book, or knew of her experiment in teaching. Without her, the Indians would certainly have fared even worse than they did. Never inflaming her people against the

Sarah's sister, Elma Smith, taken late in her life. At the time of Sarah's death she was visiting Elma.

whites, she had fought for their rights with the white man's own weapons—the tongue and the pen. Even in her last tragic years she brooded over her tribe. At an Indian "fandango" (celebration) she made a speech urging them to be "good, sober and industrious," and to get an education. She wrote a letter to the Indians of Inyo County, California, urging them to support the school there.

"A few years ago you owned this great country," her letter said. "Today the white man owns it all, and you own nothing. Do you know what did it? Education . . . You have brains same as the whites, your children have brains . . . I entreat you to get hold of this school, and give your support by sending your children, old and young, to it; and when they grow up to manhood and womanhood they will bless you."

Sarah established the first Indian school taught and managed by the Indians themselves. She wrote the first book published in the English language by an Indian, an important book of lasting value. Even today, after almost one hundred years, when it is checked against government reports and other accounts, it stands up remarkably well. Historians still refer to it, and it has recently been reissued as a paperback.

Scout—warrior—writer—lecturer—lobbyist—teacher —few people of any race have lived such a life. Her friend, Elizabeth Peabody, described it well.

She called Sarah the Indian Joan of Arc.

Bibliography

This is not a complete bibliography of works on Sarah Winnemucca and the Paiutes. It includes only those I have used and found helpful.

PRIMARY SOURCES
(Original letters, reports, etc.)

BOOKS

Angel, Myron. *History of the State of Nevada*. Oakland, California, 1881.

Annual Reports of the Commissioner of Indian Affairs. 1852–1892. U.S. Government publications.

Fremont, John Charles. *Report of the Exploring Expedition to the Rocky Mountains in the Year 1842 and to Oregon and North California in the Years 1843–1844*. Washington, D.C., 1845.

Howard, O. O. *Famous Indian Chiefs I Have Known*. New York, 1908.

Howard, O. O. *My Life and Experience Among Our Hostile Indians*. Hartford, 1907.

Meacham, A. B. *Wigwam and Warpath*. Boston, 1875.

Peabody, Elizabeth. *Sarah Winnemucca's Practical Solution of the Indian Problem.* Cambridge, 1886.

Peabody, Elizabeth. *Second Report of the Model School of Sarah Winnemucca.* Cambridge, 1887.

Winnemucca, Sarah. *Life Among the Piutes: Their Wrongs and Claims.* Boston, 1883.

Wright, William. (Dan DeQuille, pseudonym.) *History of the Big Bonanza.* Hartford, 1876.

MANUSCRIPTS

Bancroft *Scraps.* Volumes 92, 93, Set W. The Bancroft Library.

Buckland, Samuel S. *Indian Fighting in Nevada.* 1879. The Bancroft Library.

Cradlebaugh, William M. *Nevada Biography.* 1883. The Bancroft Library.

Hays, Benjamin. *Scrap Books,* Vol. 42. The Bancroft Library.

Jennings, William. *Carson Valley.* The Bancroft Library.

Klein, Jacob C. *Founders of Carson City.* 1883. The Bancroft Library.

Letters Received by the Office of Indian Affairs, 1824–1881. National Archives, microfilm. Rolls 917, 919, 920. Microcopy 234.

Martin, Thomas S. *Narrative of Fremont's Expedition in 1845–66.* The Bancroft Library.

Nevers, Samuel A. *Nevada Pioneers.* 1883. The Bancroft Library.

Prowers, Mrs. J. W. *Indian Depredations.* The Bancroft Library.

Reese, John. *Mormon Station.* The Bancroft Library.

Selected Correspondence and Papers from the Utah Super-
intendency File, 1860–1870. Record Group 75. U.S.
Bureau of Indian Affairs, The National Archives. Microfilm.

U.S. National Archives, Special File 268. *The Case of Sarah
Winnemucca.* Special Files of the Office of Indian Affairs, 1807–1904, M 574, Roll 74. Microfilm.

White, Brigadier General Jay L. *History of the Nevada
Militia, 1862–1912.* Office of the Adjutant General, Carson City, Nevada.

Winnemucca, Sarah. *Letter from Camp McDermitt, Nevada,
to the Commissioner of Indian Affairs.* The Bancroft
Library.

PERIODICALS

Boston Evening Transcript. 1883–1884.

The Council Fire. Volume VI, VII, 1883.

Daily Alta California (San Francisco) 1860–1879.

Daily Evening Bulletin (San Francisco) 1860.

Daily Silver State (Unionville, Nevada) 1875–1879.

Evening Gazette (Reno) 1882–1885.

Evening Star (Washington) 1880.

Grass Valley Telegraph (Grass Valley, California) 1853–
1858.

Hawley, A. H. "Lake Tahoe," in *Nevada Historical Society
Papers,* Volume I (1913–1916).

Hazlett, Mrs. Fanny G. "Reminiscences of Dayton," in
Nevada Historical Society Papers, Volume III (1921–
1922).

Morning Call (San Francisco) 1879–1886.

Mountain Democrat (Placerville, California) 1857, 1860.

Nevada Historical Society Papers. Third Biennial Report, 1911–1912.
Oregonian (Portland) 1879–1880.
Reese River Reveille (Austin, Nevada) 1884–1886.
Sacramento Bee 1857–1860.
Sacramento Daily Union 1857–1861.
San Francisco Chronicle 1879.
Territorial Enterprise (Virginia City, Nevada) 1858–1875.
Washington Post 1880.

SECONDARY SOURCES

BOOKS

Bancroft, H. H. *History of Nevada, Colorado and Wyoming.* San Francisco, 1889.

Bancroft, H.H. *History of Utah.* San Francisco, 1889.

Brimlow, George. *Harney County, Oregon, and Its Range Land.* Portland, 1951.

Brink, Pamela J. *The Pyramid Lake Paiute of Nevada.* Dissertation, Boston University, 1969. Published on demand.

De Voto, Bernard. *The Year of Decision, 1846.* Boston, 1943.

Dictionary of American Biography. Vol. XIV, XX. New York, 1928–36.

Downs, James F. *The Two Worlds of the Washo.* New York, 1966.

Egan, Ferol. *Sand in a Whirlwind. The Paiute Indian War of 1860.* Garden City, N.Y., 1972.

Elliott, Russell R. *History of Nevada.* Lincoln, Nebraska, 1973.

Forbes, Jack D. *Nevada Indians Speak.* Reno, 1967.

Harnar, Nellie Shaw. *History of the Pyramid Lake Indians 1852–1959.* Thesis, University of Nevada, 1965. Unpublished.

Hermann, Ruth. *The Paiutes of Pyramid Lake.* San Jose, California, 1972.

Hodge, Frederick W. *Handbook of American Indians North of Mexico.* New York, 1959. Two volumes.

Hulse, James W. *The Nevada Adventure.* Reno, 1972.

Inter-Tribal Council of Nevada. *Life Stories of Our Native People.* Salt Lake City, 1974.

Inter-Tribal Council of Nevada. *Numa: A Northern Paiute History.* Salt Lake City, 1976.

Jackson, Helen Hunt. *A Century of Dishonor.* Minneapolis, 1880.

Johnson, Edward C. *Walker River Paiutes: A Tribal History.* Salt Lake City, 1975.

Lillard, Richard G. *Desert Challenge, an Interpretation of Nevada.* New York, 1942.

Lyman, George D. *The Saga of the Comstock Lode.* New York, 1934.

McNamee, Mary Dominica, S. N. D. de N. *Light in the Valley. The Story of California's College of Notre Dame.* Berkeley, 1967.

Mack, Effie Mona. *History of Nevada.* Glendale, California, 1936.

Mack, Effie Mona and Sawyer, B. W. *Our State Nevada.* Caldwell, Idaho, 1940.

Richey, Elinor. *Eminent Women of the West.* Berkeley, 1975.

Scott, Lalla. *Karnee, A Paiute Narrative.* Reno, 1966.

Sisters of Notre Dame. *In Harvest Fields by Sunset Shores.* San Francisco, 1926.

Steward, Julian Haynes and Voegelin, Erminie Wheeler. *The Northern Paiute Indians.* New York and London, 1974.

Turner, Katharine C. *Red Men Calling on the Great White Father.* Norman, Oklahoma, 1951.

Wheat, Margaret. *Survival Arts of the Primitive Paiutes.* Reno, 1967.

Wheeler, Sessions S. *The Desert Lake: The Story of Nevada's Pyramid Lake.* Caldwell, Idaho, 1967.

Wheeler, Sessions S. *The Nevada Desert.* Caldwell, Idaho, 1971.

Wheeler, Sessions S. *The Black Rock Desert.* Caldwell, Idaho, 1979.

PERIODICALS

Brimlow, George. "Life of Sarah Winnemucca." *Oregon Historical Quarterly,* Vol. 53, June, 1951.

Egan, Ferol. "Here in Nevada a Terrible Crime." *American Heritage,* Vol. 21, June, 1970.

Egan, Ferol. "Victims of Justice, Tragedy at Carson City." *American West.* September, 1972.

Egan, Ferol. "Warren Wasson, Model Indian Agent." *Nevada Historical Society Quarterly.* Vol. 12, Fall, 1969.

Ruhlen, Colonel George. "Early Nevada Forts." *Nevada Historical Society Quarterly.* Vol. 7, Summer, Fall, 1964.

Stewart, Patricia. "Sarah Winnemucca." *Nevada Historical Society Quarterly.* Vol. 14, Winter, 1971.

Winnemucca, Sarah. "The Pah-Utes." *The Californian. A Western Monthly Magazine.* Vol. VI, September, 1882.

Index